The Eternal 'Today'

Archimandrite ZACHARIAS (Zacharou)

The Eternal 'Today'

JOURNEYING WITH THE CHURCH, IN THE LIGHT OF THE FEASTS

STAVROPEGIC MONASTERY OF ST JOHN THE BAPTIST

ESSEX 2019

The Eternal 'Today'

JOURNEYING WITH THE CHURCH, IN THE LIGHT OF THE FEASTS

First Edition © 2017 The Stavropegic Monastery of St John the Baptist, Essex, UK

Second Edition, Enlarged and Improved © 2019 The Stavropegic Monastery of St John the Baptist, Essex, UK

ISBN 978-1-909649-30-9

Designed and edited by Sister Cassiani

All photographs © The Stavropegic Monastery of St John the Baptist, Essex, UK and Mark Edwards

All images reproduced in this book come from private archives and are covered by copyright.

Published by The Stavropegic Monastery of St John the Baptist, Tolleshunt Knights, by Maldon, Essex, CM9 8EZ, UK

Printed in Greece by Lyhnia A.E.

Cover: Christ Seated upon a Rainbow, detail of The Last Judgment
Page 7: Prophet Elijah Praying in the Cave

Contents

Introduction 13

For unto us a Child is born, unto us a Son is given (Is. 9:6-7)

Thy Virtue, O Christ, has covered the heavens 21

The Theophany of our Lord 39

The Presentation of the Lord in the Temple ....…………... 49

Triodion: A Season of Spiritual Renewal

Acclimatising to the Holy Atmosphere of Great Lent 63

Sunday of the Publican and the Pharisee 67

Sunday of the Prodigal Son 71

Sunday of the Last Judgment 73

Sunday of the Expulsion of Adam from Paradise 75

Great Lent: The Feast of the Love of God

Journeying through the Sundays of Great Lent 85

Finding the Deep Heart during Great Lent 91

Sunday of Orthodoxy 103

Sunday of Saint Gregory Palamas 111

Sunday of the Cross 113

Sunday of Saint John of the Ladder 115

The Feast of the Annunciation 119

Sunday of Saint Mary of Egypt 123

Lazarus Saturday 126

Palm Sunday: The Entry of our Lord into Jerusalem 131

Holy Week: 'It is Time for the Lord to Act' (Ps. 119:126)

Holy Monday 137

Holy Tuesday 139

Holy Wednesday 141

Holy Thursday 143

Holy Friday 147

Holy Saturday 155

Holy Pascha: The Resurrection of our Lord and God and Saviour Jesus Christ

Holy Pascha: The Resurrection of our Lord and
God and Saviour Jesus Christ 163

Pentecostarion: Waiting for the Promise of the Father (cf. Acts 1:4)

'That your joy might be full' (Jn. 15:11) 173

Thomas Sunday 179

Sunday of the Myrrh-bearers 185

Sunday of the Paralytic 189

Mid-Pentecost 193

Sunday of the Samaritan 197

Sunday of the Blind Man 201

The Wondrous Ascension of Our Lord, Prophetical Event of His Glorious Second Coming 209

The Fathers of the First Ecumenical Council 213

The Feast of Pentecost 219

Monday of the Holy Spirit 225

Three Gifts of the Holy Spirit 229

Sunday of All Saints 233

Epilogue, The Eternal 'Today' of the Church 239

Index of Illustrations 244

Introduction

O ur book is a journey through the liturgical landscape that extends from the feast of Christmas until Pentecost. Beginning with the Incarnation of the Son of God, the divine work of the salvation of the world, it continues with the luminous feasts of Holy Theophany and the Presentation of the Lord in the Temple, reaching the rich liturgical period of the devotionary Triodion. The uppermost crown of our journey is Easter, during which we become partakers of the grace of the saving Resurrection of Christ. At this point a new path of expectation and desire opens up to us, leading to the great and final feast of Pentecost.

The feast of Pentecost is the fulfilment of the economy of the Lord Jesus for the salvation of the world. The Holy Spirit comes to the world to perform a great work, to seal the truth of the Lord with perfection, to witness that Christ is the true God and Saviour of the world and to guide man into the fulness of His love. The Holy Spirit opens the eyes of the soul to see the traces of the path of the Lord and to follow Him faithfully. Thus the mind is enlightened to perceive the fire of His word, and the heart is strengthened to invoke His Holy Name, as this is the calling of every Christian. When we bear the Holy Name of the Lord Jesus, then He will open up not only all the paths of our life, but also the gate of heaven, so that we can enter into the great festival of God.

Our journey reaches its end with the Sunday of All Saints. When the Holy Spirit came to dwell in the Church, the greatest fruit which was imparted were the Saints. The main work of the Church is to produce images of Christ. But who is Christ? He is the New Adam, Who came, suffered and ascended the Cross having only one thought and one desire: to save the whole world. When He vanquished death, was resurrected and ascended to heaven, He was glorified with all the content of His heart. This is the splendour of the sacrifice of the Lord, of the New Adam, and from Him come all the holy chosen people of God, who will abide for ever in heaven.

The Lord carried within Him all the nations. He died, showing His love to the end, in order to save all mankind. Thus also the Saints who are imitators of Christ, have the same 'enlargement'. They embrace through their prayer all the people of the earth, from the beginning of creation until the end of the ages. This grace of the Saints is an enlargement that flows from the incarnate God's sacrifice. As St John the Evangelist writes, we cannot say that we love God, if we do not love our fellows. If we love Him, He will enlarge our heart with love that makes room for all mankind. The Church teaches that time is neither a linear succession of events nor cyclical, but both a spiral and linear movement towards eternity. From the perspective of the history of salvation, time is a precious gift of God to man. It is the place of the meeting of the Creator and His creatures, which has been prepared so that a personal and dynamic relationship between them may develop which begins in the present life and continues into unceasing eternity.

God descended to earth and even to the nethermost parts of the earth in order to save us, and from there He ascended to the heavens. We Christians have the honour and privilege to follow Christ on the path of His descent so that later we may enter into the glory of His Second Coming. According to Elder Sophrony: 'If we really do Christ's bidding, all that He went through will be repeated in us, be it to a lesser degree.'[1]

The Church commemorates the saving work of Christ, which He performed 'once and for all' and remains active for all time. When we participate in feasts, we do not merely journey in time in our mind, but we receive a real taste of eternity while still dwelling in a specific place and time.

In every feast of the Church we are able through the grace of the Holy Spirit to meet Christ already from this present life and to experience the past, present and future all at once. In this way, the meaning of time takes on a new dimension that we could characterise as an eternal present, time overshadowed by eternity, a gift of the Church to her light-bearing children.

1 Archimandrite Sophrony (Sakharov), *On Prayer*, trans. Rosemary Edmonds, Stavropegic Monastery of St John the Baptist, Essex, 1996, p. 100.

For unto us a Child is born,
unto us a Son is given!
Is. 9:6-7

Nativity Troparion

Thy Nativity O Christ our God
Hath shone upon the world
with the Light of knowledge,
for thereby they who adored
the stars, through a star
were taught to worship Thee,
the Sun of Righteousness
and to laud Thee,
the Dayspring from On high,
O Lord glory Thee!

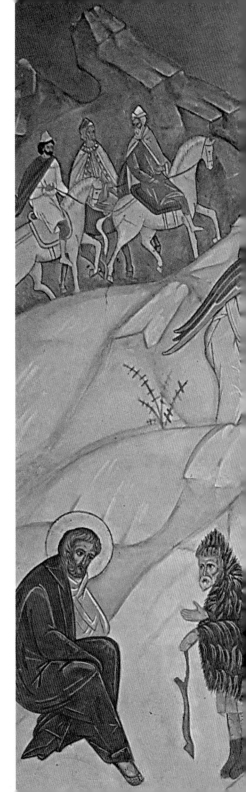

Thy virtue, O Christ, has covered the heavens [1]

W ondrous is the event of the Nativity of Christ and perfect the grace of this feast, which spreads over the earth. The virtue of Christ covers the heavens and the Holy Church shines from gladness at the coming of the Most High into the world. It joyously celebrates the manifestation of the love of God, Who so loved the world, that He gave His Only-begotten Son, that whosoever believes in Him should not be lost in the darkness of non-being, but have everlasting life. [2]

God became Man, as the Fathers say, so that man might become god. The Most High descended from heaven, so that man might ascend from his fall. God became poor so that poverty-stricken man might become rich. At Christmas, we celebrate the new creation, the 'regeneration'[3] and refashioning of man. From the moment when God was born and brought grace to earth, the Church, as a mother in travail, suffers anguish and birth pangs, longing for the Son of God to be born in the heart of every man who believes.

On the day of Christmas, we celebrate the birth of Jesus Christ. This is the greatest mystery of godliness, as the Apostle Paul says,

1 Matins of the Meeting of our Lord, Irmos of Canicle 4, (Festal Menaion, p. 421). Cf. Hab. 3:3.
2 Cf. *John* 3:16.
3 Cf. *Titus* 3:5.

'that God was manifest in the flesh'.[1] At the same time, we celebrate yet another event, namely, that men have received 'grace upon grace'.[2] That is, from now on men have the potential to be born in the Spirit together with Christ and born again through His grace.

This is the hope-bearing message of the feast of the Nativity of Christ, the Lamb and Shepherd,[3] as He is called in the Akathist Hymn. For He is the Lamb Who shepherds the shepherds, and the Shepherd, Who shall gather all together in His Kingdom, lambs and goats, wolves and sheep.

According to the Gospel, the Nativity of the great Lamb and Shepherd happened in Bethlehem,[4] the city of His ancestors according to the flesh. This was the glorious city of David, the great King of Israel. It was meet that Christ be born in Bethlehem, for He was the seed of Abraham and the descendant of King and Prophet David. He Who would become the true King of kings[5] and would reign over all the earth arrived there, due to the wise providence of God and the decree[6] of Caesar. He Who would later become the Governor of Israel, was born in Bethlehem.[7] And who is Israel? Certainly, there is the historical people of Israel, but there is also the spiritual Israel. In Hebrew, Israel means 'the mind which beholds God'.[8] In other words, the Christians who gaze at the Invisible God through faith are the holy nation,[9] the holy Israel of God.

---

1 *1 Tim.* 3:16.
2 Cf. *John* 1:16.
3 See the Akathist Hymn, Oikos 4, Lenten Triodion, p. 425.
4 See *Matt.* 2:1.
5 *1 Tim.* 6:15.
6 *Luke* 2:1.
7 *Matt.* 2:6.
8 Cf. *Gen.* 32:24–30.
9 See the Divine Liturgy of Saint Basil, Prayer of Anaphora.

What a great and strange wonder: the 'King of the Jews'[1] came to Bethlehem and could find no place to stay. The 'Lord of lords'[2] came into the city of His ancestors as a refugee. Through the misery of their migration, the refugees offered a homeland, the heritage of His family, unto Him, of Whom every 'family in heaven and earth is named',[3] as the Apostle Paul says to the Ephesians.

From the dawn of the life of the divine Infant we discern the unspeakable mystery of the self-emptying of the Son and Word of God. Incomprehensible and indescribable is His greatness, infinite and unfathomable His descent. It is impossible for us to conceive of the grandeur of God with our earthly mind, and we lack the strength to apprehend His humility and His descent, because the God of Christians, the Lord of Israel is boundless in the wealth of His divinity and perfect in His immeasurable searchless self-emptying.

What inference can we draw from the vulnerable way in which Jesus was born without anyone apprehending Him? Whoever has ears to hear,[4] eyes to see, and a heart to understand, perceives that for as long as man lives in this world possessing it, enjoying it, being satisfied and satiated by it, Christ cannot be formed in his heart. This vain world makes every effort to leave its impressions on our soul, fighting to enslave our mind through its idols and to keep hold of us through ephemeral images which it tries to imprint as deeply as possible within us. This world stirs up passionate desires, which, when satisfied, generate greater passions, creating a great tumult in the heart, even the Babylon of the passions. The Prophet says, 'O

1 *Matt.* 2:2.
2 *1 Tim.* 6:15.
3 *Eph.* 3:15.
4 *Matt.* 11:15; *Mark* 4:9; *Luke* 8:8.

daughter of Babylon, who art to be destroyed: happy shall he be, that taketh and dasheth thy little ones against the stone.'[1] That is, blessed is the man who crushes the onset of thoughts and passions on the rock of faith.

Seeing the miracle of the birth of Christ which happened in the most humble and vulnerable way, nothing remains but for us to also become strangers to this world. This is in fact what we are taught by the verse of the Akathist Hymn: 'Seeing this strange birth, let us become strangers to the world fixing the mind in heaven.'[2] We will become strangers to the vanity of this world which lies in wickedness, only when we transfer our mind to heaven for 'our conversation is in heaven',[3] there where Christ is and where our life is hidden.

The great Apostle Paul says: 'Brethren, when Christ, who is our life, shall appear, then shall ye also appear with him in glory.'[4] In other words, now we must hide our life in Christ. We live in this transient world with our body, but with our mind we transfer all our life to heaven. This world will not become for us the 'continuing city',[5] but we shall live as sojourners on earth, imitating the Most Holy Mother of God and her betrothed Joseph, who were sojourners in Bethlehem. We must be but passing guests in this world, if we want to give Christ space in our heart to be born. We must not have a continuing city here, but seek the 'one to come', as the Apostle exhorts us in his Epistle to the Hebrews.[6]

1 Cf. *Ps*. 137:8-9.
2 Akathist Hymn, Kontakion 8.
3 *Phil*. 3:20.
4 *Col*. 3:4.
5 *Heb*. 13:14.
6 Ibid.

Abraham received a great promise from God that through him all the nations of the earth would be blessed. Christ brought this blessing to all the nations, 'Go ye therefore, and teach all nations.'[1] Discipleship and regeneration in Christ are not a natural birth, but a spiritual birth by the grace of God. It is a birth 'not of blood nor of the will of the flesh, nor of the will of man, but a birth of God'.[2] God gave man the power of recreation and regeneration according to his faith. If Abraham did not leave his homeland with faith, if he did not abandon his kin and become a refugee, he would not have received the glorious covenant, the great promises and the unbelievable inheritance, that in his seed all the nations of the earth would be blessed. Abraham went into this exile with faith and was justified, 'By faith he sojourned in the land of promise, as in a strange country.'[3] Through faith and absolute trust in God, he journeyed to the land which God had shown him, and lived there as a foreigner in a strange country, dwelling only in tents. We read in Scripture that he dwelt 'in tabernacles with Isaac and Jacob, the heirs with him of the same promise: For he looked for a city which hath foundations, whose builder and maker is God.'[4] Abraham did not build palaces, he did not make his permanent abode on the blessed land, which God had shown him, but expected another city, which would have different foundations and whose builder and creator is God.

The clear-sighted Rebecca cast out her innocent son, Jacob, saving him from his vengeful brother Esau.[5] If Jacob had not fled out of obedience to his mother and with faith in God, he would not have

---

1 *Matt.* 28:19.
2 See *John* 1:13.
3 *Heb.* 11:9.
4 *Heb.* 11:9-10.
5 See *Gen.* 27.

come to that awesome place where he dreamt about the future event of the Incarnation of Christ.[1] Jacob saw the heavenly ladder which united heaven and earth, that is, he knew prophetically the mystery of the Mother of God, the Gate of heaven. The Holy Virgin became the bridge which brought God from heaven to earth and man from earth to heaven.[2]

Furthermore, if Israel did not elect to suffer and endure hardship in the desert for forty years with faith, accepting the unknown path of Yahweh, then the Lord of Hosts would not have come with all His angelic powers to build up His tabernacle among His chosen people and to have His eyes always open towards the temple of Solomon night and day.[3]

The people of Israel received the greatest revelations in the desert, where they did not have 'a continuing city', but sought with great pain the destination which God had promised them. In a similar way, the greatest revelations are given to the new Israel in the noetic desert, where man is not attached to anything vain and fleeting, but cleaves with his spirit to the uncreated and eternal God, having his gaze fixed only upon Him.

The word 'Bethlehem' has two meanings: the house of God and the house of bread. The Lord Jesus is both. He is the Almighty God, and the 'the bread of God which cometh down from heaven, and giveth life unto the world.'[4] This bread is given only to those who are rejected in this world. As the Apostle Paul writes, God has

1 See *Gen.* 28:10-22.
2 Akathist Hymn, Oikos 2.
3 See *1 Kgs.* 8:29.
4 Cf. *John* 6:33.

chosen the weak things of this world, the lowly, the 'despised'[1] and the 'filth',[2] these things has He blessed and covered with His grace, that He might be glorified even more. Through His Incarnation, Christ made king once more the wretched and despised man, desiring that we come to know that all our being is on loan from Him. Everything we have is a gift of His goodness and we owe Him the deepest gratitude.

Only those who become voluntarily marginalised and poor in this world, imitating Him Who 'for our sakes became poor',[3] will be blessed by the Lord. Such are those who become poor for Christ's sake, above all with spiritual poverty, keeping vigilance and inner attention.

In the Book of Proverbs it is written, 'Keep thy heart with all diligence; for out of it are the issues of life.'[4] This means that life and death arise from the thoughts of our heart. The lives of the Saints speak about the guarding of the heart and the mind, because from the heart spring forth all expressions of life. If wicked and evil thoughts emerge from our heart, then we deliver ourselves to death: 'For the wages of sin is death'.[5] If, however, we purify our heart and cultivate good dispositions, then we tread upon the 'paths of life'.[6]

Through His birth, the Lord concealed His infinite eternity, the lightning of His Divinity, and accepted to assume the name Son of the carpenter,[7] as the Jews called Him. The true King of kings

1 Cf. *1 Cor.* 1:27-28.
2 Cf. *1 Cor.* 4:13.
3 Cf. *2 Cor.* 8:9.
4 *Prov.* 4:23.
5 *Rom* 6:23.
6 See *Ps.* 16:11
7 *Matt.* 13:55.

concealed His majesty and made a manger His throne, the hay His riches, and the illiterate shepherds the first servants of His Kingdom. They were the first to see and hear the glory of the Lord, and they became witnesses of this awesome event. The infinite God, the 'Ancient of days' became a Babe, and concealed His divine wisdom and almighty power within the weakness of His infancy. No matter how much we try, our mind fails to comprehend this strange mystery. The Lord covered His perfect Divinity with the weakness of an infant, showing us that becoming a child is the way which leads to the blessedness of Divine power, to the wealth of His Kingdom. But what kind of child? That kind which the Apostle Paul teaches us, 'Brethren, be not children in understanding: howbeit in malice be ye children.'[1] Let us then be without guile in our childlikeness. The highest wisdom is to deny one's own understanding, to become a fool for Christ's sake through faith. Then we will see the foolishness of God transformed into 'the power of God and the wisdom of God'.[2] When we crucify our mind for the sake of God's commandments, we become babes, 'fools for Christ'[3] and we are vouchsafed to receive the Lord in our heart, as the Holy Virgin received the Son of God. The lower we descend in humility – if, to be sure, we do not fear to descend – the higher we will be raised by God.

The immaculate Mother of the wondrous Infant says that the quality which God discerned in her and for which He magnified her was her humility. 'For he hath regarded the low estate of his handmaiden'[4] and 'he that is mighty hath done to me great things'.[5]

1 *1 Cor.* 14:20.
2 See *1 Cor.* 1:24.
3 *1 Cor.* 4:10.
4 *Luke* 1:48.
5 Cf. *Luke* 1:49.

When Mary lived in the Temple in the Holy of Holies studying the Scriptures, she found the passage of the Prophet Isaiah, which says: 'Behold, a virgin shall conceive, and bear a son, and shall call his name Immanuel.'[1] Her mind stood still at this thought and from that moment she prayed with all the fervour of her heart that God may vouchsafe her to become the handmaid of the woman who would bring Emmanuel into the world. While praying in this manner, she received the answer through the word of the Archangel Gabriel: 'Hail Mary full of grace, the Lord is with thee.' 'For thou hast found favour with God.'[2] What a wondrous and incomprehensible thing! Through the extreme humility of her spirit, the young maid became the greatest minister of the mystery of the God's Incarnation and of the salvation of men. It is proper to God to create from nothing. However, two foundations are needed for Him to build His temple within us:[3] humility and self-denial. The deeper these two stones are set, the higher and more magnificent becomes the temple of God within us. When we acknowledge and confess our nothingness, then we become known of God[4] and suitable material for recreation, 'laying up in store for ourselves a good foundation against the time to come'.[5]

One further characteristic of the Nativity of Christ is the purity of His spotless Mother. The purity of the Mother of God was never tarnished by any corruption, not even by a gesture or a thought. Mary had as her betrothed, the righteous Joseph.[6] The Apostle Paul

1 *Isa.* 7:14.
2 Cf. *Luke* 1:28-30.
3 Cf. *1 Cor.* 3:16.
4 Cf. *1 Cor.* 8:2-3.
5 Cf. *1 Tim.* 6:19.
6 *Matt.* 1:19.

explains that 'the law is not made for a righteous man'.[1] Therefore, in the language of Holy Scripture, 'righteous' denotes the deified man who is above all natural laws and lives beyond every carnal thought. Therefore, the characterisation of Joseph as 'righteous' is a sufficient assurance that he was an holy man.

God ordained for the Mother of God to have the righteous Joseph as her betrothed, so that he might be a witness to her purity, and at the same time, her protector. The Mosaic Law decreed that any unmarried girl who brought a child into the world should be stoned to death. Thus, through this betrothal, God ensured that the Holy Virgin be protected and that the righteous betrothed bear witness to the truth of her purity. The Fathers teach, furthermore, that God chose this path so as to show that the Nativity of Christ was not to be understood as a condemnation or belittling of blessed marriage, but rather as its exaltation.

Let us consider the purity of the Mother of God, whose beauty was perceived and desired by the King.[2] We know from the Old Testament that our God is a jealous God.[3] He is not contented only with a part of man's heart but He thirsts for the whole of it. He is not well-pleased when man's love is divided, because He Himself gives all things to man, 'All that is mine is thine.'[4] God gives Himself wholly to us and awaits in return our whole heart. He says, 'My son, give me thine heart.'[5] The beauty of the virginity of the Mother of God is beyond compare. 'The Mother of God never sinned even

---

1 *1 Tim.* 1:9.
2 *Ps.* 45:11.
3 *Ex.* 20:5.
4 *Luke.* 15 :31.
5 *Prov.* 23 :26.

in thought', Saint Silouan teaches us.[1] Every distancing from God, even in man's thought, is considered spiritual adultery, as unbelief and as a fall. For this reason God gave the commandment: 'Do not commit adultery.' This commandment should not be understood on an ethical level, but on a spiritual one. The heart of man should not be separated from God by even one vain thought.

This is what the Saints achieved in their lives through the cultivation of unceasing noetic prayer. Through prayer they found a practical way to live continually with their whole being immersed in the quickening presence of God, abiding inseparable from Him. If it is continuously and persistently turned towards heaven, the heart is cleansed and sees God. 'Blessed are the pure in heart for they shall see God.'[2] But where do they see God? Not in icons, neither in nature nor in flashes of lightning, nor in the signs and wonders of the times, but mainly and most distinctly, in their heart. The more transparent the heart becomes, the clearer the image of Christ will also become within it. For just as pure water and shining crystal reflect the sun, so also the heart of man, as a clean mirror, reflects the glory of the great King, the image of Christ.

If we wish to be reborn through the grace of Christ Who is now being born in the flesh, we must be exercised in spiritual virginity, which is the unceasing abiding of the mind in God, through vigilance and the guarding of the heart. We should surrender our whole heart so that He Whom nothing can enclose might dwell therein, although God is always greater than our heart.[3]

1 Archimandrite Sophrony (Sakharov), *Saint Silouan the Athonite*, trans. Rosemary Edmonds, Stavropegic Monastery of St John the Baptist, Essex, 1991, p. 392.
2 *Matt.* 5:8.
3 *1 John* 3:20.

If we desire to be united with Christ, we must guard our heart in every possible way, in all haste, with all watchfulness and attention, because, as we already mentioned, out of the heart come the issues of life,[1] but also of death. The Bridegroom of the Church unites Himself with those who are without blemish and pure, and is a stranger to those who out of despondency slumber and sleep before His Bride Chamber.[2] God made a great feast, He prepared a rich supper and invites us. We must not be despondent and darkened by the cares of this world, but respond to the invitation with burning 'lamps',[3] otherwise our sleep may well become the sleep of death.[4] When the soul is pure and turned towards God, it is able to apprehend spiritual life, which is the blessedness of the vision of God.

Notwithstanding, let no fear assail us because we do not live like strangers in this world, because we are not like unto children and have not the utter humility and spiritual virginity, which we find in the Nativity of Christ and in His Most Holy Mother. Let our mind be darkened by no despair, but on the contrary, let us contemplate the hymn of the Angels at Christ's Birth, 'Glory to God in the highest, and on earth peace, good will toward men.'[5] The Angels sang the glory of God, Who brought all things into being, and they sing the same hymn every time we repent. There is great joy in heaven when we return like the prodigal son to the Father. Then Angels praise again the glory of God's grace, which led the sinner to return and be born anew. They sing the peace that was restored between man and

---

1 See *Prov.* 4:23.
2 *Matt.* 25:12.
3 *Matt.* 25:8.
4 *Ps.* 13:3.
5 *Luke* 2:14.

his Creator. They sing, 'I bring you good tidings of great joy,'[1] for every day is a beginning of repentance for whosoever is firmly established in the hope that, 'joy shall be in heaven over one sinner that repenteth'.[2] Jesus was 'the expectation of the gentiles',[3] now He is their only hope. For in the God of those who repent, 'shall the Gentiles trust'.[4] 'A multitude of the heavenly host'[5] perpetually glorify the Incarnate Love which accepts our repentance at every moment.

The shepherds, though insignificant in the eyes of the world, hastened to venerate Christ and were united in the hymn of His Nativity; let the same happen for us all, who long for a new birth 'of water and of the spirit'.[6] The Holy Spirit will be our bond, which will unite us in one Body, the immaculate Church, and will give us a communion of life, where each one will treasure, help, comfort and strengthen the other. Then as holy 'members one of another',[7] we shall all hymn the wonders and the glory of God, as the Angels in heaven at the hour of the Nativity.

The Magi, the wise kings of the East, brought unto Jesus gifts of gold, frankincense and myrrh.[8] Let us also bring as a gift the renewal of the royal priesthood,[9] which Christ granted us through His precious Blood, making us 'kings and priests unto God the Father'.[10] We are kings when only Christ reigns within us, when we are

1 See *Luke* 2:10.
2 *Luke* 15:7.
3 See *Gen.* 49:10 (LXX).
4 *Rom.* 15:12.
5 *Luke* 2:13.
6 *John* 3:5.
7 *Rom.* 12:5.
8 *Matt.* 2:11.
9 *1 Pet.* 2:9.
10 *Rev.* 1:6; 5:10.

free from all that is alien to His Spirit. Then we partake of the royal ministry of Christ and 'death no longer hath dominion over us',[1] but full of the Holy Spirit we minister unto our own salvation and unto the salvation of the whole world. Let us not neglect 'so great a salvation',[2] but on the contrary, with abundant inspiration and desire, let us go to meet the Divine Infant. At the time of the Nativity of Jesus, Herod became mad with rage and Jerusalem was thrown into chaos. It is the same in our times: the princes of this world stir up conflict and the nations are at war. As for us, the Lord has hidden us in a secluded place within His tabernacle, as David says, 'In the secret of his tabernacle shall he hide me.'[3] Our life is hid with Christ in God,[4] it is hidden and stored in heaven, because wherever Christ is, there is our life also.

Perceiving with gratitude, my dear brethren, the wondrous dispensation of the Love of God, which traverses the tragic history of mankind, striving at 'sundry times and in diverse manners'[5] to restore man to the beauty he had in the beginning, let us prepare ourselves this Christmas to glorify God verily and in truth, 'in our body and in our spirit'[6] through our sanctification.

Let us create on this afflicted earth a small remnant of the descendants of Jesus, the children of the New Adam, who will bear witness with their lives that 'unto us is born a Saviour, which is Christ the Lord',[7] Who will come again to 'judge the world in righteousness'.[8]

1 See *Rom.* 6:9.
2 See *Heb.* 2:3.
3 *Ps.* 27:5
4 *Col.* 3:3.
5 *Heb.* 1:1.
6 *1 Cor.* 7:34.
7 Cf. *Luke* 2:11
8 *Acts* 17:31.

Theophany Troparion

When Thou o Lord

wast baptised in the Jordan,

the worship of the Trinity

was made manifest;

for the voice of the Father

bore witness unto Thee

calling Thee the beloved Son

and the Spirit in the form of a dove

confirmed His word

as sure and steadfast;

O Christ our God

Who hast appeared

and enlightened the world,

glory to Thee!

The Theophany of our Lord

'To those that sat in darkness a bright dawn has appeared'[1]

At the feast of Theophany, Jesus Christ is revealed as the beloved Son, the Son of the good pleasure of the Father. We have just celebrated His coming in the Flesh. We worshipped Him as a new-born Babe and Son of the Virgin. Today, however, His humble appearance in the Jordan is sealed by the witness of the heavenly Father. The Prophet Elijah did not know God in the thunder, in the storm or earthquake, but in the still small voice of calm; thus also now, the Son of man comes meek, humble and quiet, accepting to be baptised by the Righteous Forerunner. Yet God the Father also manifests His good pleasure for the Only-begotten Son: 'This is my beloved Son, in whom I am well-pleased.'[2]

The baptism of the Righteous Forerunner was directed towards the people and had a preparatory character, aiming to refashion at least in part the customs of men, to train them not to put their faith in external acts of cleansing, to perceive the need for repentance and thus to prepare for the meeting with the Coming Lord. As for the Baptism of Christ, it is the revelation of 'the mystery, which was kept secret since time began,'[3] the mystery of the Holy Trinity. In the baptism of John, we

1 Ikos, Matins of Theophany.
2 *Matt.* 3:17.
3 *Rom.* 16:25.

find ourselves under the threat of the coming wrath of God. The Forerunner speaks hard words to the Jews in order to crush the cruel arrogance of their hearts of stone, and in this way he attracts the grace of consolation to them.[1] The Baptism of Christ, however, is the brilliance of Divinity, witnessing to His divine coming. John stirs up our conscience that we are 'children of Abraham',[2] whilst the Almighty Jesus, through His Baptism, is straitened to restore us as sons of God. The Apostle Paul writes that Christ 'descended first into the lower parts of the earth'.[3] Thus His descent into the waters of the Jordan is a foreshadowing of His descent into Hades. The Lord came and united the Light of His Life with all creation, sanctifying the waters and the whole universe by His Baptism. He came and filled every aspect of life with His divine energy, so as to grant us the possibility to meet Him and to find grace under any circumstances whatsoever, whether we find ourselves in great joy or in deep despair. 'The Light of His Countenance shines upon the world and to those that sat in darkness a bright dawn has appeared'.[4]

We see that both forms of baptism follow the preaching of repentance. First John calls to repentance by warning of the 'wrath to come' and that the Kingdom of God draweth nigh. The preaching of repentance of Christ Himself follows, which is the presupposition of His Gospel and works by the Light of His Countenance. The first had as his purpose to 'prepare the

---

1 *Luke* 3:18.
2 *Matt.* 3:9.
3 *Eph.* 4:9.
4 Ikos, Matins, Theophany.

way of the Lord',[1] while the second to show us the ontological chasm which separates us from the incarnate Christ, and thus to inspire another kind of repentance, which does not just bring the Kingdom of God nearer, but establishes it within us.[2]

The Light of the Countenance of the Lord attracts every soul to Him and inspires repentance on an ontological level, crossing the distance between man and God, a distance that is bridged only through the energy of Divine Grace.

The collaboration of our repentance is a necessary presupposition to receive the gift of the Holy Spirit, but it is also the only path to preserve divine grace. This is why we also repent before our baptism,[3] so as to conform our life to the Holy of Holies, Whom we long to 'put on' in the holy Sacrament. During Baptism, we repent and denounce the darkness of this life, so that the covenant which we concluded with Christ is engraved even more deeply in our consciousness. The character of this covenant lies in that henceforth we will not live for ourselves, but only for Him. We will be dead to sin and the passions and live only for God.[4]

During our immersion in the water, we meet and put on Christ, and then we enter into 'newness of life'.[5] However, we need repentance even during the baptism, because sin so easily besets and wounds us. In the Gospel of Luke the Lord

1 See *Matt.* 3:3.
2 See *Luke* 17:21.
3 We are discussing the baptism of adults, but this is also true in the baptism of infants, when repentance should be offered by the initiating priest and the godparents of the child.
4 *Rom.* 6:11, 8:10.
5 *Rom.* 6:4.

instructs us that even if we have fulfilled all the command-ments, we must say to ourselves, 'We are useless servants, we have done that which was our duty to do.'[1] Therefore, we need repentance and humility after Baptism as well, due to the commandment of God, so as to keep the gift which we received, 'perfecting holiness in the fear of God'.[2] In reality, the feast of Theophany has a dual meaning, witnessing to the first appearance of Christ, which occurred in a secret and concealed way, and prophesied His Second Coming which is yet to happen at the end of the ages. Christ is 'the One Who has come and is Coming again to judge the world in righteous-ness',[3] and through His Incarnation He becomes Himself the prophet of His Second Coming. During His Baptism, when He descends humbly into the Jordan, the Heavenly Father and the Holy Spirit testify to His divine origin, disclosing the eschatological dimension of His submerging. This is shown also in the apostolic reading of the feast, which begins by describing the first appearance of the Lord, saying, 'For the grace of God that bringeth salvation hath appeared to all men. Teaching us that, denying ungodliness and worldly lusts, we should live soberly, righteously, and godly, in this present world.'[4] In the following verse, the Apostle turns his mind to the Second Coming of Christ, so as to be: 'Looking for that blessed hope, and the glorious appearing of our great God and Saviour Jesus Christ.'[5]

1 *Luke* 17:10.
2 See *2 Cor.* 7.1.
3 See *Ps.* 9:8, 96:13, 98:9, and *Acts* 17:31.
4 *Tit.* 2:11-12.
5 *Tit.* 2:13.

The same eschatological perspective can also be detected in many of the other events in the life of the Lord. First of all, His birth already revealed something about His Second Coming. The Lord 'was born secretly in a cave'[1] and legions of angels surrounded him saying, 'Glory to God in the Highest and on earth peace, good will to all men.'[2] The same can be observed also in the Transfiguration, when Christ revealed His uncreated glory to His three chosen disciples, forty days before His Passion. Furthermore, during the terrifying time of the awesome Golgotha, the earth shook and the sun was darkened and covered its rays. That is to say, many things happened, which Prophet Joel had said would occur at the Second Coming.[3]

This eschatological spirit seals the Resurrection of the Lord together with His Ascension, when the angels cry out to the Apostles: 'Ye men of Galilee, why stand ye gazing up into heaven? This same Jesus, which is taken up from you into heaven, shall so come in like manner as ye have seen him go into heaven.'[4] In the end, the last things become present, above all, in the great and final feast of Pentecost, when the flame of the Comforter transforms the disciples into vessels of the Holy Spirit and renders them taught of God. At Pentecost, we already see the realisation of that which was prophesied for the Last Judgment , when Christ will reign in glory, and no one will need to teach his brother about God, because all will

1 See the troparion of the Nativity of Christ.
2 See *Luke* 2:14.
3 See *Joel* 2:10.
4 *Acts* 1:11.

become taught of God: One will be the Teacher, Christ and the personal relationship with Christ will transmit to the saved the knowledge of God, a knowledge which will never diminish.

We see therefore that through the Incarnation of Christ, the last things are at work already in history. For us it remains to assume the life that Christ revealed to us, and the only path towards this is repentance. We must have the Countenance of Christ always before our eyes, in order to make the attraction of the love of Christ which He brought upon earth a reality, according to His word: 'And I, if I be lifted up from the earth, will draw all men unto me.'[1] Just as in Baptism so also in the Liturgy, the Countenance of the One Who, 'though He was rich' in glory and divinity, 'became poor' for our sakes,[2] is revealed to us, and we must seek to be pleasing to Him and make it the purpose of our life that whether 'present or absent, we may be accepted of him'[3] so that we may thus 'ever be with the Lord'.[4]

The ontological repentance that is begotten within us by the vision of the Countenance of the Lord knows no end on earth, and the humility which accompanies it is indescribable. Thus, the 'threat' that Saint John the Baptist used to crush arrogance and bring consolation is therefore no longer needed. By contrast, as Saint Silouan bears witness, the vision of the indescribable humility of Christ is enough for our heart to render all its space to the Lord.

1 *John* 12:32.
2 See *2 Cor.* 8:9.
3 *2 Cor.* 5:9.
4 See *1 Thess.* 4:17.

In the dialogue that takes place between the Holy Forerunner and the Lord, we can discern a competition as to who will humble himself more before the other. The great John, who humbled the Jews by calling them, 'children of vipers',[1] humbled himself before Christ, Who was 'without blemish and without spot',[2] saying 'I have need to be baptised of thee, and comest thou to me?'[3] These words reveal the spiritual grandeur of the Holy Forerunner. The Jews bore John the deepest respect and considered him a great prophet and teacher. However, when he saw Christ approaching, he recognised Him and immediately set at His feet all the honour which he himself had enjoyed from the people, saying 'He must increase, but I must decrease.'[4]

This is the gratitude of the servant towards the Master, even if here the servant is presented as similar to the Master. The Forerunner humbles himself and the God-man Christ humbles Himself even deeper before the Forerunner, 'Suffer it to be so now: for thus it becometh us to fulfil all righteousness.'[5] This competition is a 'spiritual law' which forms the attitude of all men who have been 'born again': if someone humbles himself before them, then they humble themselves all the more.

God did not save us by His omnipotence, but through the weakness of His love, co-suffering with us, giving us such an example, which would be well-pleasing to the Heavenly Father.

1 *Matt.* 3:7.
2 See *1 Pet.* 1:19.
3 *Matt.* 3:14.
4 Cf. *John* 3:30.
5 *Matt.* 3:15.

When we, too, become weak for His sake and turn towards Him with a painful heart, the Lord will bend down over us and overshadow us with His grace, bringing us to a new birth and bestowing on us the incomparable honour of adoption. As Scripture says, 'As many as received him, to them gave He power to become the sons of God, even to them that believe on His name, which were born, not of blood, nor of the will of the flesh, nor of the will of man, but of God.'[1]

The Lord is He Who 'is and was and is to come'.[2] Our preparation for His Second Coming begins when we bear His reproach, in other words when we cast off the bonds of the mind and values of this world, and go outside the camp with the expectation of meeting with Him.[3] This is the greatest repentance possible and the best preparation for meeting Him Who came and will come again. Repentance cleanses man through the grace which accompanies it and makes him a dwelling-place of divine illumination. All those who receive this illumination, will become children of God and like unto the Lord, because they will see Him as He is[4] and with Him they will be blessed and will reign over all the ages. 'By descending into the water (of humble repentance) we ascend to God.'[5]

1 *John* 1:12-13.
2 See *Rev.* 1:4.
3 See *Heb.* 13:13, *2 Pet.* 3:12 and *Tit.* 2:12-13.
4 *1 John* 3:2.
5 See Stichera of Lauds, Matins of Theophany.

The Presentation of the Lord in the Temple

The Mystery of Divine Consolation in Man's Heart

I n the Church, God has given us the privilege that our life
become a continual feast. We journey from one feast to another, savouring each time the blessing of the day. God hon-
ours us and cares for us continually through His grace, keeping festival with His people.

During our life on earth we enter into the presence of the Lord
in a secret, inner and heartfelt way. In heaven, however, according to the Apostle Paul, we will see the Lord face to Face.[1]
There we will abide with the Lord and converse with Him,
contemplating the ineffable beauty of His Countenance like
the first-created. Eternal life is paradise, an endless festival. Today, once more, we celebrate a feast. The day of the Presentation is uniquely beautiful, because it is a feast of the Lord and
at the same time of the Mother of God: 'When the days of her
purification according to the law of Moses were accomplished,
they brought him to Jerusalem, to present him to the Lord.'[2]
When forty days had passed after the birth of Christ, Mary
and Joseph brought the child to Jerusalem, yet there was no
need for the purification of the Most Holy Mother of God as the

1 *1 Cor.* 13:12.
2 *Luke* 2:22.

birth of Jesus was virginal and supernatural. If it had been a conventional birth, then Holy Scripture would have spoken of the purification of the mother. Instead in the original Greek it says, 'when the days of *their* purification were accomplished',[1] meaning the purification of the Jews, that is of a custom that they had under the Law of Moses.

The custom of keeping forty days of purification remained in the Church of Christ from the Jews. Studying the prayers of the Church for the fulfilment of forty days, we start to comprehend the wondrous image which the Holy Church has for the integrity and the spiritual purity of the human body. The Church does not view the woman as unclean when she gives birth, but conversely it views the body of the woman, and more generally the human body, as a temple of the Holy Spirit. During the pregnancy, if a foreign hand touches the body of the woman, even if it is by necessity, forty days are required to re-establish the purity of the body as the temple of God.

'They brought Him to Jerusalem to present Him to the Lord.'[2] The presentation of Jesus before God is a great mystery. It is the mystery of self-emptying, of the incarnation and sacrifice of the Lord, which is in essence His prophetic and holy Priesthood according to the order of Melchisedek.

Today, the Royal Priesthood of Christ begins. Today, there appears in the temple as a Babe, the One Who is the Lord of the temple presenting to us the ministry of our salvation. All

1 See *Luke* 2:22.
2 *Luke* 2:22.

that which will later be accomplished through His Cross and Resurrection takes place now in a prophetic foreshadowing. We begin, that is, to see prophetically from today the evidence and the fruits of the sacrifice of the Lord.

All that the Lord achieved through His dispensation for man is contained in His presentation, in His ministry for our salvation. Priesthood and presentation are almost synonymous. This is why the priests say in their prayers, 'Vouchsafe us to present ourselves before the throne of your grace'[1] or 'Bless our presentation.'

According to Elder Sophrony, the Lord embraced heaven and earth in one single act, through the twofold movement of His descent to the nethermost parts of the earth and His ascent to heaven, to serve the salvation of mankind. From the first moment of His coming to the world, Christ made a twofold presentation, through which He justified both God and man.

His first, downward movement is the presentation that He makes before man. Through this movement He justifies God, showing man what God's love 'unto the end' means. God gave His Only-begotten Son for our sake and through Him He grants us all things.

The second, upward movement that Jesus makes is His presentation before God the Father, through which He introduces into the Kingdom of heaven the army of the saved ones who follow Him. Jesus justifies man before God presenting

1 See *Heb.* 4:16.

Himself as the perfect man, as an example of conduct and fidelity to the word and will of God. He showed us the true man, who is acceptable to God.

Every man who follows His example, is received by the Father of spirits unto all ages.

Furthermore, the twofold presentation of the Lord brings man before God. Jesus traversed the heavens and henceforth they remain open, so that all who follow His path can enter therein.

The feast of the Presentation marks the beginning of the Royal Priesthood of Christ, through which the Lord justifies God and saves the word,[1] but at the same time it also indicates our own participation in the Royal Priesthood of the Lord. This is accomplished when the sword of repentance enters our heart so that healing waters of tears gush forth.

Lord, help us in the presentation of our repentance to glorify Thy Name and find Thy salvation.

Lord, do Thou, Who through Thy presentation hast justified God and saved the world, help us so that our humble presentation on earth may glorify Thy Name and be for the salvation of our souls.

'Now lettest Thou Thy servant depart in peace according to Thy word, for mine eyes have seen thy salvation, which Thou hast prepared before the face of all people, a light to enlighten

1 See *Heb.* 5:7-9.

the gentiles and the glory of Thy people Israel.'[1] This prayer is more beautiful even than the Psalms of David. It is the song of the triumph of a soul who has known God. This 'new song'[2] was sent up to God by the righteous Symeon, who was vouchsafed to see the 'Ancient of Days' Who is at the same time the God Who makes all things new.

This is the song of praise of the Saints of God, the hymn that will end their life in holiness. We also sing this ode at the end of Vespers and during our thanksgiving at the end of the Divine Liturgy, where we have our greatest meeting with the Lord. Symeon received in his arms the Lord, Who touches and sanctifies, touches and heals, touches and fills the house of man's soul with saving grace, so that with gratitude he confesses and declares:

'The moment that I received the Child in my hands, my every longing and desire was fulfilled. Now, Lord, release me, free me from the bonds of my body in a peaceful way and according to Thy promise, as Thy salvation is already present before my eyes. Now that I hold Thee in my arms, I understand how Thy salvation is at work in man.

Now I acknowledge, O Lord, the proof of all the prophecies about Thee, I have seen the Saviour Whom we expected, and I possess evidence of His grace in my heart. For this, O Master, free me, so as to be vouchsafed to see also in heaven the fulness of salvation, of which I now glimpse the beginning.

1 *Luke* 2:29-32.
2 *Ps.* 33:3.

That which you have begun in my heart, give me the power to endure it unto the end, so as to enter with all the power of my soul into the fulness and perfection of Thy salvation.

Now I understand, Lord, that Thou hast prepared the mystery of Thy salvation before the face of all people, I cannot but wonder at the universal salvation that Thou hast prepared for all the people of the earth.'

Today we see the righteous and devout Symeon open his arms and receive the divine Infant. The contact with the Lord enlarges his heart, so that it embraces all heaven and earth. Symeon made this salvation his own and preached its universality for all the nations which Isaiah had foretold.

In a similar way to Symeon the God-receiver, Saint Silouan beheld the Living Christ in the chapel of Prophet Elijah and all his being was filled with the fire of the grace of the Holy Spirit, which witnessed in his soul to salvation. Receiving the enlargement of grace he began to pray with longing: 'I pray Thee, O Lord, that all the people of the earth may come to know Thee in the Holy Spirit.'

'And Symeon blessed them, and said unto Mary his mother, Behold, this child is set for the fall and rising again of many in Israel; and for a sign which shall be spoken against; Yea, a sword shall pierce through thy own soul also, that the thoughts of many hearts may be revealed.'[1] Symeon prophesied the Passion of the Lord to the Holy Virgin, saying that great pain will

1 *Luke* 2:34-35.

pierce her soul, when she will see her Son crucified. A sword would pierce her soul, so as to reveal the thoughts of men's hearts.

Thus the righteous Symeon forewarned the Mother of God that she would be the first to experience the judgment of Her Son and its fruit.

On the day of the Crucifixion of the Lord all creation suffered. The spectacle of supernatural events that took place was awesome. The sun was darkened, the earth shook, tombs of the dead were opened, the veil of the temple was torn and it was unbearable to behold 'God crucified',[1] as it is said in the hymns. Even the brutal crucifiers of the Lord could not bear it, but 'smote their breasts and withdrew'.[2] The only one who stood by the Cross was the Holy Mother of God and by her side John who was of the same kind. The love that she had for the Lord, and the light of grace that dwelt within her soul, made her unshakable in this trial and the sword that pierced her heart was 'for the sanctification of many'.

A similar sword pierces the hearts of all those who desire to follow the Lord. According to the Apostle Peter, we will be tested by fire and go through a fiery furnace of pain. This will not cause us to perish, just as the Holy Virgin did not perish, but it will come to pass so that the Spirit of glory may rest within us. The fiery trial is allowed by God so that we may be unshakable in faith and that the Holy Spirit may abide constantly within our

1 See Matins of Holy Friday.
2 See *Luke* 23:48.

heart. The mystery of the Cross and the Resurrection, which worked in the soul of the Mother of God in such a powerful way, is repeated in all the faithful disciples of the Lord, who follow His path. This is the reason that the Apostle Peter says, 'Beloved, think it not strange concerning the fiery trial which is to try you, as though some strange thing happened unto you.'[1] Tribulations come to test us, so that the Spirit of glory may rest upon us.

The Lord bestows His grace and enlarges the heart of man, who is initiated into the universality of Christ and knows that the true Saviour of the world is none other than Christ. This knowledge of God is the incorruptible consolation of the new Israel, of the people of God. All those who receive divine consolation, as Symeon received it, whether they are Saints or sinners, stand before God and say, 'Now lettest Thou Thy servant depart in peace, O Master, according to Thy word.' When man has tasted the only true consolation, he can face death without cowardice or faintheartedness. Whoever is vouchsafed the enlargement of the Lord's grace is certain that 'death hath no dominion over him',[2] because he bears in his heart the Lord of life and death. This is the only way in which man can confront death without fear and set out with longing to his meeting with the Lord, singing a triumphal hymn. This is the splendour and the mystery of our meeting with the Lord, which is hidden within the feast of the Presentation of the Lord in the Temple.

1 *1 Pet.* 4:12.
2 See *Rom* 6:9.

Christ came into the world and presented Himself before God as perfect thanksgiving to Him, as perfect Man, and with this His perfect presentation He became the perfect pattern of life for man.

Triodion:
A Season of Spiritual Renewal

Acclimatising to the holy atmosphere of Great Lent

The Triodion covers every week of Great Lent, as well as the four preceding Sundays. The theme of every Sunday developed in the Triodion describes the spiritual disposition which ought to accompany the struggle of Great Lent for the renewal of Christian life.

The season of the Triodion is so important that the Church offers two other Sundays as an advance preparation: that of Zacchaeus and the Woman of Canaan. These lead us into the Triodion. The Sunday of Zacchaeus teaches us that when one desires to see the Face of Christ with one's whole being, one becomes indifferent to the opinion of society, so that being a laughing stock in the eyes of men is of no consequence. The shame which one endures, however, is transformed into strength resembling the grace of salvation.

The Sunday of the Woman of Canaan is extremely moving in its teaching. When a person shows fidelity and devotion to God, like dogs to their masters, then true contact with Christ is established. One may follow Him freely and deliberately, irrespective of whether one is tested or experiences mercy. For this faithfulness, one then receives the praise of divine adoption and inherits everlasting life.

The Triodion begins with the Sunday of the Publican and the Pharisee. Here, the Pharisee's self-justification leads to condemnation and destruction, while the humble and constrained cry of the Publican's self-condemnation attracts the blessing of God and the sinner's justification. God never despises a contrite and a humble heart.

Then follows the Sunday of the Prodigal Son, which reminds us that however much man may have distanced himself from God, He awaits him with an open and fatherly embrace. He only has to come to himself and say freely from his heart: 'Father, I have sinned against heaven, and in Thy sight, and am no more worthy to be called Thy son' (Lk. 15:21). He then wonders at the reply of Divine goodness: 'All that I have is thine' (Lk. 15:31).

Then comes the Sunday of Meatfare and the parable of the Last Judgment. Here we are informed that every deed of love towards the least of our brethren will stand next to us to justify us on the Day of Judgment. This love is humble. At the moment when God glorifies a good deed, those who have done it are astonished, seeing themselves as unworthy. Contrariwise, sinners will be confounded by unexpected torment, because of their prideful stance accompanying them even beyond the grave. The following Sunday – *Sunday of Cheesefare* – has forgiveness as its theme and refers to Adam's exile from Paradise.

We do not forget that on this earth we are exiles and once deceived. If, however, we struggle during the course of Lent which is about to begin to fulfil the customs laid down by the Church, both outward and inward, we shall find the grace of Christ's Resurrection and enter the feast of the love of God. We shall attain to this if we forgive all and do not shut anyone out of our heart. Then God will rest in us.

Sunday of the Publican and the Pharisee

The Publican

Bowing himself down to the ground, the Publican smites his chest, for he desires to enter into his heart so as to speak from there to the Lord, saying: 'God be merciful to me a sinner.'

Self-condemnation anticipates the Last Judgment, for it leads to forgiveness of sins and the justification of God Who, as a good Comforter, easily relates to those who have a contrite heart and a humble spirit, 'for whosoever exalteth himself shall be abased; and he that humbleth himself shall be exalted' (Lk. 14:11).

According to the testimony of the Saints, there is no rule of prayer more pleasing to God than the pitiable voice of the Publican, which says: 'God be merciful to me a sinner' (Lk. 18:13).

The Pharisee

Full of arrogance and haughtiness, the Pharisee says: 'God, I thank thee, that I am not as other men are, extortioners, unjust, adulterers, or even as this publican' (Lk. 18:11), and other foolish words.

Through his self-justification he estranges himself from the justice of the Lamb of God, which was expressed on the Cross: 'Father, forgive them, for they know not what they do' (Lk. 23:34), and so he separates himself from all those 'other men' receiving forgiveness, upon whom he passes judgment.

Whosoever justifies himself hates the salvation of his own soul.

Sunday of the Prodigal Son

Lord, Thou seest me in a solitary place,

moonless and desolate, abiding with swine,

the passions of my selfish will,

being entrenched with demons.

Endow me with the courage to come to myself

and behold the abyss of my degradation,

that I may return to Thee,

entering into the banquet of joy and love,

the honour of Thy Divine adoption.

Sunday of the Last Judgement

Whoever justifies himself accuses himself. He hates the salvation of his soul and shall be surprised by unexpected tribulation on the day of the Second Coming of the Lord.

Whoever blames himself shall not be judged. He shall be surprised by unanticipated bliss on the day of the Lord and be immersed in an endless depth of gratitude for his eternal salvation.

The first shows the behaviour of sinners in this life which continues so in the world to come.

The second is the attitude of the righteous on earth which will accompany them for all eternity.

Sunday of the Expulsion of Adam from Paradise

Today we are reminded of the Paradise of God that we lost, of the honour that we have received from our Creator to be fashioned after the image and likeness of God, Who endowed us with a deep heart, able to bear within it the living and wondrous sensation of His presence. Our communion with the true God is for us the bliss of Paradise.

At Vespers we already start seeking for ways to return to Paradise, to the fulfilment of our pre-eternal destiny. The spotless Church of our God reminds us that, because of the sin that preceded, we find ourselves here on earth cast out from His Paradise, and we sorrow grievously for being bereft of its gladness. From Saint Silouan's words we learn that Adam and all the saints of God, in their sensitivity and purity of their hearts, sought the lost Paradise with a mighty lamentation:

'O Paradise, my Paradise, my wondrous Paradise!
Where art Thou, my Lord?
Why hast Thou hidden the beauty of Thy face from me?
What hinders thee from dwelling in me?
O, why did I grieve my beloved God?
My soul yearns after Thee and I seek Thee in tears.'
(From *The Writings* of Staretz Silouan)

And so, the very Lord and King of Paradise Himself came to earth and assured us that His Kingdom is within us (cf. Lk. 17:21), in our hearts, and that without His grace we can do nothing. Thus, according to Christ's word, our life on earth has now only one programme, only one purpose, which is to find out how to return to our God, and acquire His grace so as to retrieve our lost Paradise, that is, life-giving communion with our beloved Creator.

The first step on the way of our return to God is revealed to us in today's Gospel reading: we must begin by forgiving all from our heart. Saint Silouan tells us that we truly forgive our brethren when we pray for them as we pray for ourselves. Such forgiveness opens our heart to the grace of God. The Lord loves us so much that He laid down only one condition for our life, that we should be forgiving in equal manner to Him. Thus if we forgive men their small and relative offences, He will of a surety grant us in His turn perfect and absolute forgiveness, that we may be with Him for ever. It is forgiveness that creates in our heart a space for our brother so that we may receive him in our heart as our life. As soon as we forgive, the Lord begins the work of His eternal salvation in us. He gives us the first portion of His grace, which is to believe in His word and love His promises.

Such faith which 'worketh by love' (Gal. 5:6) reveals unto us our own heart, which awakes from its age-old sleep of sin and is filled with the living sensation of the presence of God. Such faith becomes the light of life. At the same time we are filled with wisdom from another world, with the wisdom of humble thoughts, which rekindle our desire of union with God. We begin to see more clearly which things grieve our beloved God, and which things are pleasing unto Him Who redeemed us with His precious Blood. And thus we discover that there are many hidden and deceitful things in us which do not delight our Lord, but grieve His Spirit.

Then we are given the second portion of God's grace, which is greater and more powerful. We make a new beginning of repentance for God to cleanse our heart, so that it may bear without hindrance the presence of the Lord. Gradually, the grace of God purifies the heart, imprinting on it the image of the Lord and making it resound with His strange and wondrous word. The spiritual struggle gains intensity and zeal so as to cleanse this space, which is the holy temple of God, the dwelling-place of the Holy Spirit. Man then draws nearer to God and follows Him more faithfully, wherever He may lead him. And God rewards his striving by granting him even greater grace, which enlarges his heart to embrace heaven and earth in his love. Then man is united with God and with all humanity, which becomes the content of his heart. He prays fervently and intercedes before God for the salvation of the whole world.

We see, therefore, that unless we forgive with all our heart, we shall neither be vouchsafed to love God as He deserves and as we owe Him, nor shall we find true Paradise. For the heart which truly loves the Lord cannot suffer that a single soul should perish. If we continue in resentment against our brother, this shall in time grow into hatred. And hatred can become uncontrollable, that is, able to make us in the likeness of the author of hatred, which is the devil, even the murderer of men.

All the spiritual exercises that the Church offers to her children during Great Lent have this purpose of enabling man to find his deep heart (cf. Prov. 20:5) so that, from there, he may turn towards God with all his strength and perform all things with his heart.

If man has discovered his deep heart, then, when he believes, he will believe with all his heart and orientate his whole life towards Him in Whom he believes. He will accept Him as his Saviour from Heaven and rewarder for his deeds. Then faith becomes a holy gift and man loves Him in Whom he believes. When he prays, he will speak unto God with tender desire, with all his mind and with all his heart. Then God will hearken unto him and grant him His reward. When he studies the word of God, man will strive to hear it resounding in his heart in order to become familiar with the language of God, so that on the glorious day of His Second Coming he may recognise His voice from within his heart, as a praise of His salvation.

When he repents, man will cry from his heart and with fear, seeking forgiveness for his sins, whether known or secret. He will take upon himself the shame for his own sins, and render justice and glory to the God of mercy. The Lord will then reward such humility by granting His grace unto him and enlarging his heart. When he loves God and his fellow-men, he will love them humbly with his heart, without any desire 'to appear unto men' (Mt. 6:16), for his endeavour is to save all the space of his heart for his beloved God and his brethren. Then it is that man begins to fulfil the commandment of love in a manner worthy of God.

When he fasts, when he gives alms or prays, he will do these things humbly and without grudging, again, so as 'not to appear unto men' (Mt. 6:16). Then God, Who sees the secret work of his soul, will strengthen his heart and give him greater zeal. The more he preserves himself from the pestilence of vainglory, the more he will progress spiritually. And the more he will bear within himself the dying of the Lord Jesus, the more the life of the Resurrection of the Lord Jesus, now risen from the dead, will abound in his heart.

If the grace of this holy period that is about to begin is so great, then it is truly worth showing our forbearance and forgiving all our fellow-men of like passions with us. Let us, therefore, humble ourselves before God and before our brethren, seeking for a place of repentance and for the mercy of God.

Let us give thanks then, from our heart to the Lord, Who gives us Great Lent with its holy atmosphere in which we have the possibility to be baptised once more and to find spiritual regeneration, so as to hear again in our heart the voice of the Lord, to see His image imprinted in it and to be able to stand in the sacred presence of our Risen Lord. May we also be vouchsafed our personal Passover, that is, our passage from death unto life, and life endless and eternal.

Great Lent:
The Feast of the Love of God

Journeying through the Sundays of Great Lent

Having now entered the period of Great Lent, on the First Sunday of Lent, the Sunday of Orthodoxy, God permits us to test Him and to know Him. However, we must approach Him without deceitful prejudices. Then we are convinced and believe that Christ is the Son of God, the King of the new Israel, which is the Church. Correct faith in Christ leads us to the marvel of the union of Heaven and Earth. This is a powerful and never-ending wonder, in which we shall see 'greater things than these' (Jn. 1:50), according to the Lord's promise. From this moment we also, grateful for being strengthened in God, shall continually chant a new song (cf. Ps. 149:1), a hymn of gratitude and humble love.

Journeying towards the Second Sunday of Lent, the Sunday of Saint Gregory Palamas, we are now around forty days before Easter. If we were in the early Church we would be feasting the Lord's Transfiguration, but the Church in her wisdom moved this feast to the 6th of August, forty days before the feast of the Exaltation of the Precious Cross. In its place, we celebrate the memory of Saint Gregory, the extoller and theologian of the Divine Light of the Lord's Transfiguration. The blessed vision of this uncreated Light is the fruit *par excellence* of a right faith in the Divinity of Christ, without which all ascetic labours are in vain.

On the Third Sunday of Lent, in the very middle of Great Lent, we venerate the Precious and Life-Giving Cross. The Lord's Cross is exalted as a manifestation of His perfect love for the world, and the purpose of the feast is to renew our inspiration and patient endurance in the struggle, till we arrive as well at the joy of His Resurrection. The Cross of Christ is indescribably great and embraces the tragedy and pain of all creation and every age. Yet, His inheritance is infinite and eternal. Christ urges us to bear our Cross with self-denial and follow Him. In comparison, our cross is very small. It is the suffering of some ill which Divine Providence lovingly and discretely accords us, in order to free us from every tie and attachment, that with a free heart we may love our benefactor, God, and run His way faithfully and steadfastly. The small cross which we bear in fulfilment of His commandment becomes the key to the eternal inheritance which Christ gained for us by His Great Cross.

We continue the journey of this period of contrition to the Fourth Sunday of Lent, the Sunday of Saint John of the Ladder. In remembering this saint, the Church declares that a holy life is the fruit of one's cross in friendship with God. The book of *The Ladder* by Saint John of Sinai is a masterpiece which shows the stages in spiritual life and perfection in a life of holiness. It begins with the first step of exile for the sake of God and reaches the steps of perfection, divine dispassion and love. It comprises the treasure of the Church's knowledge on the precise way of the Lord.

Arriving at the Fifth Sunday of Lent, the Sunday of Saint Mary of Egypt, we approach the end of Great Lent. Now the Church encourages us with the example of Saint Mary. She witnesses that however much man may be drowning in sins and passions, even if he goes down to the depths of hell, he should not despair because he can meet Christ everywhere and become like an angel, as did Saint Mary. Repentance truly can raise man from the abyss of hell to the Heaven of heavens.

This is why in the middle of this week, in order to extend her prayer of repentance, the Church chants *The Great Canon* of Saint Andrew of Crete. In this canon, the saint employs Holy Scripture in a panoramic way. The word of God becomes the word of prayer of repentance on an ontological level, in which the one who repents lives the whole of Sacred History as though it were his own personal experience. He possesses prophetic self-knowledge which crushes him and causes him to hate sin, yet at the same time, he is inspired by the way of the humble and meek Lord who desires that all may be saved. He repents for the whole world and his repentance becomes a superhuman event which brings him up to the level of divine existence, together with all the Saints of heaven: 'Attend, O heaven, and I shall speak; give ear, O earth, to the voice

of one who repents before God' (*The Great Canon* of Saint Andrew of Crete).

Christ descended from Heaven to earth. His humility and compassion brought Him down to the nethermost parts and to hell, so that through the Divine action of His presence, He may be there present and alive. However low we may fall, we still have the possibility of meeting Him. Our life can be made new again, so that we may ascend to Heaven with Him, sharing into the triumph of life over death, which He, as Saviour of the world (cf. Jn. 12:47), gained for us.

The Church instituted Great Lent in order to help us discover our 'deep heart' (Ps. 64:6). To aid in this struggle, the Church offers us various exercises: mutual forgiveness, repentance, spiritual mourning, prayer, fasting, the word of God, holy hymns, works of humble love and forbearance in brotherly love, and much more. All of her services are laden with deep and heavenly thoughts which keep our mind captive to God alone. When we succeed in turning with our whole heart to Him, He then makes us radiant and grants us to partake in His continuous and grace-filled presence, entering into the feast of His undying love.

Finding the Deep Heart during Great Lent

T he grace of God gathers us together in the Church, at the beginning of Great Lent, so that we might express to the Lord our longing for the acquisition of the spirit of wisdom and understanding of His commandments.

Holy Scripture, however, warns us: 'It is impossible for a heartless man to get wisdom' (Prov. 17:16). What is the 'heart' for us as Christians, and what kind of person can be called 'heartless'? The heart of every one is fashioned by God in a special and unique manner (cf. Ps. 33:15). It is unrepeatable and makes up the core of the human hypostasis.[1] Man becomes truly great when he draws near to God with his 'deep heart' (Ps. 64:6), because there, within him, is 'the place of spiritual prayer'[2] and the 'battle-ground of spiritual struggle'.[3] True theology and knowledge of God are inseparable from the sensation of the deep heart. This is why the word of God assures us that the 'hidden man of the heart' is 'of great price before God' (1 Pt. 3:4).

1 See Archimandrite Sophrony (Sakharov), *We Shall See Him as He Is*, trans. Rosemary Edmonds, Stavropegic Monastery of St John the Baptist, Essex, 2004, pp. 84, 196.
2 *On Prayer*, p. 11.
3 *Saint Silouan the Athonite*, p. 10.

The calling of the Lord is addressed to man's heart, 'the spiritual centre of the person'[1] which has the ability to lay hold of eternity, so that he might 'recognise his Prototype – the Living God'.[2] A man who cannot feel his heart has, in the place of the luminous dwelling-place of God, just a pump that sends blood to the body. He is heartless, he cannot acquire wisdom. Only when man has a divine and noetic sensation in his heart (cf. Prov. 15:14) is he truly alive before God. Otherwise his nature is divided: his heart seeks one thing, his scattered mind another, while his unbridled body obstinately pursues the satisfaction of its needs and passions. When the mind is separated from the heart, it is dispersed through its senses into the created world, 'tossed to and fro, carried about with every wind' (Eph. 4:14) of imagination and easily captivated by demonic energy and delusion.

Without being guarded by the governing mind at its threshold, the heart remains hardened; its earth brings forth only evil thoughts, which drown the incorruptible seed of the word of God (cf. Heb. 6:8; 1 Pt. 1:23). It becomes, then, a den of every vice. Sin, as a spiritual event, is committed secretly in the depth of man's heart.

If our body and our spirit are to become a place of the manifestation of the glory of God, so that we may truly celebrate our personal Easter, we need to find our deep heart. The mind scattered in vain and mindless cares must return

1 *We Shall See Him as He Is*, p. 174.
2 *Ibid.*, p. 194.

and unite with the 'body most interior to our body'[1], our heart. The Holy and Immaculate Church, treasure house of gifts of the Holy Spirit, sets out the period of the Holy Fast as a light which shines likes the dawn, illuminating and redeeming the remaining time of our life. Great Lent is for us a great opportunity, a privilege, which God gives us to cooperate with him, in order to re-ignite the grace which we received through Holy Baptism and to quicken our heart.

This period helps us to offer our own small part to God, for example in the fulfilment of the commandment of fasting. Fasting humbles our body and spirit so as to make space in the heart for the visitation of grace. This grace unites us with the other members of the Church, so that we may also become partakers of the gifts of its stronger members, the Saints. According to Father Sophrony, fasting refines the heart and makes it 'clairvoyant'[2] through grace and able to receive spiritual wisdom. Saint Silouan teaches in the same spirit that fasting is beneficial, when combined with abstinence, watchfulness, stillness and other virtues. Its main power is, however, drawn from humility.

In the beginning of the healing process recommended to us by the Church during the Lenten period, the mind, having been gathered up from the world where it is dispersed through the senses, enters into the heart.

---

1 Saint Gregory Palamas, *The Triads,* C, 1, ii, 3, New Jersey, 1983, p. 43.
2 *We Shall See Him as He Is*, p. 99.

The mind unites with the heart in a new vision: God becomes the centre of all things and man humbly turns towards Him. The spirit of repentance dredges our depths and makes manifest that which is concealed within our heart. Then we see our true state as if through the eyes of God. Just as sin is committed in the depth of the heart, so repentance also occurs in the heart, the innermost place of our spirit. Repentance heals and strengthens our nature through the grace of God and gives birth within us to an uncontainable surge of longing for God.

During Great Lent the Holy Church endeavours to instil and intensify in us a strong impetus towards repentance, through fasting, rich services inspiring contrition, prostrations, bending of the knees and all of her other exercises. The Church's purpose is to inspire burning prayer, which purges us from the passions and sows within us the holy pain of divine love, so that neither in our mind nor in our heart will there be left any other thought than hatred for the sin that so easily besets us and flaming desire for the Saviour God. The central point of such repentance is to keep the covenant which we made at our Baptism that, from now on, we will be dead to sin and alive to His word and commandments. During Holy and Great Lent the Church desires to make us partakers of the word of the Lord, 'I was dead, and behold, I am alive forevermore' (Rev. 1:18), giving us the opportunity to receive a small taste of death through fasting, confession, giving alms and, more generally, through asceticism.

By means of suffering during Lent, we become like unto and kindred to Christ Who is suffering in this world (cf. Acts 26:23). The power of His Resurrection is imparted to us, so that we, as light-bearing children of the Church, may sing on the chosen and holy day of Easter: 'Yesterday I was buried with Thee, O Christ. Today I arise with Thee in Thy resurrection. Yesterday I was crucified with Thee: Glorify me with Thee, O Saviour, in Thy kingdom' (*Paschal Canon,* Ode 3). In the measure in which we participate in the suffering and self-emptying of Christ, we shall also receive the wealth of His gifts and the grace of His Resurrection.

One further way in which we can find our deep heart during Great Lent is through the continual reading of Holy Scripture. The word of Christ is uncreated Divine Light, which is directed to the deep heart of man, the core of his hypostatic principle.

First of all, in order that our heart may open to the word of Christ and receive the grace of repentance, we must have complete faith in the Divinity of Christ. Then the living word of Christ will fall into the hidden depth of our heart as a seed of love which gives birth in our soul to repentance surpassing the measure of ordinary religious conscience.[1] This experience powerfully convinces us that the teaching of Christ exceeds the level of the ethical and is deifying. The evangelical teaching illumines our inner vision with the resplendence of the word of God and refines a spiritual sensation within our heart, so that

1 See *Ibid.,* p. 194.

from now on not one movement or thought escapes our attention. Abiding in the word of the Lord enables us to observe His Divine commandments and thus to place ourselves on the way of the Lord, and He, Who is Himself the Way, becomes our fellow traveller. If we abide in the evangelical word with thirst and fortitude, then, just like Luke and Cleopas, we shall acquire a heart which burns within us (cf. Lk. 24:32), ready to receive and recognise the Risen Lord by the fire and sweetness of His love. The mind descends into the heart, is healed and united with it when it is crucified through the Gospel commandments. Overshadowed by grace, we are able to renounce all the visible things of the world and to become disciples of the spirit of the incorruptible love of Christ.

The union of the mind with the heart becomes possible through a crucifixion which occurs in two phases.

In the first phase, when, according to the Apostle Paul, 'the world is crucified unto me...' (Gal. 6:14), a great struggle is undertaken to escape the vanity of the world and enslavement to its lofty prototypes which are an abomination before God. In the second phase, '... and I unto the world' (Gal. 6:14), all our effort is concentrated in surrendering ourselves completely to the will of God, uprooting the law of sin from our heart and freeing ourselves from our inner slavery. The spiritual battle continues until the Gospel word is inaugurated within us as the sole and eternal law of our being.

Saint Dorotheos of Gaza and Saint Gregory Palamas interpreted this passage of the Apostle Paul, 'The world is crucified unto me and I unto the world' (Gal. 6:14), applying it to the two stages of crucifixion in the life of the monk. Both Fathers also connect the first phase with the renunciation of the sin that so easily besets us in the world, and the second to the inner death of man to sinful passions, that is to say, to dispassion.

Then we become the temple of God, and we bear within us as a guest the Spirit of grace, no matter in which external circumstances we may live. All creation becomes for us a Church and a place of presentation before the Living God.[1]

Father Sophrony discerned in these two stages two degrees of spiritual freedom. The first degree is our renunciation of the world and relinquishment of power over others. The second degree is perfect freedom of heart which is essential if we are to stand immovable in the presence of the Lord. This is to 'unshackle oneself from the authority of others'.[2] The perfection of man's freedom is his perfection as a person. This is our perfect fulfilment and our final purpose.

How can we avoid sin living in the world which 'lieth in wickedness' (1 Jn. 5:19)? It is possible only if we learn to live with our heart, accusing ourselves in prayer of repentance and keeping vigilance by invoking the name of the Lord.

---

1 See *Saint Silouan the Athonite*, p. 294.
2 *We Shall See Him as He Is*, p. 115.

Through watchfulness, we will find a 'well of water' (Jn. 4:14) and light in the heart which attracts the mind. Malicious suggestions or images will not imprint themselves in the mind and heart, but will easily be despised, because the attraction of the inner man towards the heart will be stronger than any external impressions: 'Because greater is he that is in you, than he that is in the world' (1 Jn. 4:4). Without watchfulness, grace cannot be retained in the heart. Spiritual mourning keeps us in constant contact with the Spirit of Life, until the grace of God that accumulates in the heart reaches its fulness. Finally, our new birth in the Holy Spirit is realised.

Christ through His Cross and Resurrection fulfilled the great commandment which He received of His Father (cf. Jn. 10:18) and gave to the faithful 'grace upon grace' (Jn. 1:16). The person who invokes the Name of Jesus is initiated into the mystery of the Cross and the Resurrection of Christ, and his heart is brought to life and becomes a temple of Divinity. The godly invocation of the Name of Christ quickens the presence of the Eternal God in our heart and imparts to us an especial energy, like a new life which permeates all our being. The repetition of the Name of Christ not only ceases to be burdensome, but leads us to an increasing plenitude of love and wisdom. Our eyes are opened so that we continually discover new mysteries of the way of Christ and of His unfathomable providence within our everyday life. We are enriched with the experience of eternity.

The season of fasting is a time of work on our heart and a school of voluntary death. The way of the Lord passes through the death on the Cross and the descent into the netherworld of hell unto the life-bearing Resurrection.

As we take on voluntary suffering, accepting the trials which the providence of God allows in our life without grudging and with gratitude, we explore through faith the unspeakable mystery of Divine Love, which reaches for our sake into the very depths of hell. Our knowledge of the mystery of Christ will never be complete, if our experience does not contain also the descent into hell.

Faith in the Resurrection of Christ and hope in our own resurrection inspire us to live in accordance with the commandments of God, dead to the will of our flesh. Thus our deep heart will emerge and we will know from experience that we have been transported 'from death to life with Christ Jesus' (Eph. 2:6).

Only that work which we have wrought within our heart will accompany us into eternity. If we cleanse our heart in this life, then in accordance with the promise of God, we will see His Countenance: 'Blessed are the pure in heart for they shall see God' (Mt. 5:8). The tragedy of contemporary man is that he lives outside his heart. He thinks, works, speaks, and even loves and prays, outside his heart.

This period of Great Lent gives us Christians a great opportunity to enter into our heart and return to it like the prodigal son to his Father's house. The vision of our inner hell in the light of the holiness of God and the fervour of His spotless love provokes in our soul an unrestrainable desire 'to break out of the chains of our fall'[1] and surrender entirely to the God of light and love, who comes to give life and not death. Then the voice of the Lord will resound in our heart: 'My son give me your heart' (Prov. 23:26) and the same will proclaim, 'Thou art my son, this day have I begotten thee' (Ps. 2:7).

Through His living word the Lord Jesus sowed an incorruptible seed (cf. 1 Pt. 1:23) and by the grace of His Spirit He granted us the gift of adoption (cf. Eph. 1:5), giving birth to the Church and making us children of His Resurrection. The victory of Christ over the last enemy, death (cf. 1 Cor. 15:26), is accomplished in our deep heart and there the triumph of the Orthodox faith also takes place. In other words, grace will imprint upon our heart the image of the Lord Jesus and will make us heirs of His victory over death.

Let us give thanks to God, Who gives us this sacred time of Great Lent, permeated by His grace, so as to help us to find our deep heart and to enter into the living presence of Christ, risen from the dead. Christ, the Bridegroom of the Church (cf. Lk. 5:35), knocks at the door of our heart (cf. Rev. 3:20), seeking the perfect union of our soul with His Holy Spirit.

1 *We Shall See Him as He Is*, p. 22.

Each time we approach Him and enter His wondrous presence is our own Easter. Let no one who has faith remain outside of the Bridal Chamber of Christ. Having faithfully followed all the ordinances described for the period of Lent and experienced its spiritual benefits, may we all celebrate an eternal Easter, as a time of renewal and a landmark of grace.

Sunday of Orthodoxy

On the Sunday of Orthodoxy we celebrate the restoration of the true practice of venerating icons, according to the teaching of Saint John of Damascus (c.675 - c.749) against the Iconoclasts.[1]

Salvation is the cooperation of two factors: Divine and human. The first is infinitely great, the second infinitely small, but absolutely necessary. The Sunday of Orthodoxy states what Orthodoxy is, namely, a harmonious cooperation between God's revelation, given through the Prophets, the Apostles and the Saints and our small contribution of faith in all that God has revealed and given us, along with a surrender of our will to God's will, so that the icon of the Heavenly Man, Christ, be formed in our hearts. Thus we become temples of the Holy Spirit, not built by human hands (cf. 2 Cor. 5:1) but by Divine grace.

This formation of the inner icon of Christ in our hearts is the Triumph of Orthodoxy over our fallen nature, over our passions, and over the machinations of the evil one and the spread of false teachings (cf. 1 Tim. 6:3).

---

1 The Iconoclastic controversy lasted from 726, when Emperor Leo III (717-741) contested the use of Icons as holy images in Christian worship until 843, when the Empress Theodora proclaimed their restoration.

On the first Sunday of Great Lent we celebrate the triumph of Orthodoxy, that is, of the true revelation of God which was 'once delivered unto the saints.'[1]

'Following our fathers', we, too, are possessed with the desire not to lose anything, not even one jot from the life-bearing word of the Lord. The Church sets forth the teaching of the right faith so as to renew the inspiration of her children, which must unfailingly accompany them throughout the struggle of this period, so that they may reach the desired end, their entrance into the life-giving presence of the Risen Christ. Without the right faith in the Divinity of Christ, all things become relative, and the longing for reconciliation with God is blunted and slackens. Any attenuation of the truth of God that has been handed down to us cannot possibly give birth to holiness of life.

At sundry times and in divers manners',[2] God gives us on the one hand the revelation of His truth, which is His spotless love, and on the other hand of the truth of man, as He conceived of it before the foundation of the world and manifested it in the last days in the Person of His Son. In the Old Testament, man is defined as a deep heart seeking for a spiritual and divine sensation.[3] He is also defined as the 'target of God',[4] because, according to Job, from morning until evening and from evening until morning, God visits man and makes him the target of His loving care. God longs to give to His

1 See *Jude* 1:3.
2 *Heb.* 1:1.
3 See *Prov.* 15:14 and Saint Gregory Palamas, *Triads*, 1, 3:3, 20-21.
4 See *Job* 7:20.

creature all that is His, to speak to him as to His equal and to establish him as His true image, able to collaborate in the fulfilling of His divine will for the salvation of the whole world.

In the New Testament, according to the word of the Apostle Paul, the ultimate purpose of man's creation and his great destination is that he become the dwelling-place of Divinity, the temple of the Living God.[1] Hence, the ardent prayer of the Church is that the image of Christ be formed in her members[2] and that the Lord may dwell in their hearts by faith.[3] In the weakness of human flesh that Christ assumed, He revealed the perfection of the Father without Beginning, and He is our only example in every aspect of our life. Following in His footsteps we can acquire this perfection which God foreordained for us.

Therefore, Orthodoxy is first of all the right revelation about God which was given to us by Christ, and, furthermore, the right way of life, the perfection of life that this revelation inspires, as the practical fulfilment of the commandments. According to the word of the Lord, it is the keeping of the commandments that transforms the heart of man from flesh into a luminous dwelling-place of the Holy Spirit. 'If a man love me, he will keep my words: and my Father will love him, and we will come unto him, and make our abode with him.'[4]

In other words, there is a difference between simple faith in the revelation which was delivered to man and the faith which

1 See *1 Cor.* 3:16, *1 Cor.* 6:19, *Rom.* 8:9, *Eph.* 2:22.
2 See *Gal.* 4:19.
3 See *Eph.* 3:17.
4 *John* 14:23.

makes man deliver himself to the will of God with unwavering confidence in His gift. Revelation makes manifest unto us the Hypostasis of the Son and Word of God and, above all, its inner content, which is His love 'unto the end',[1] as it was sealed by the shameful death of the Lord on the Cross. 'For God so loved the world, that he gave his only begotten Son, that whosoever believeth in him should not perish, but have everlasting life.'[2] This knowledge begets in man the inspiration to respond to Divine goodness with a sense of honour and gratitude, and to strive to imitate the example of Christ by keeping His commandments. The Lord gave us these commandments, not in order to annihilate our personality and deprive us of our freedom, but as a means of healing our nature, which has been wounded by sin and death, so that we may repossess our true spiritual freedom.

According to His promise, The Lord did not leave us orphans,[3] but gave us the means to reach our destination. He left us His Name as an inheritance, 'the name of the Lord Jesus which is above every name, before which every knee should bow, of things in heaven, and things in earth, and things under the earth',[4] the only Name under heaven through which we are given the possibility to work our salvation.[5] Moreover, He revealed unto us His quickening word, which is not at the measure of man, neither invented by man.[6] His Gospel is Divine

1 See *John* 13:1.
2 *John* 3:16.
3 See *John* 14:18.
4 *Phil.* 2:9-10.
5 See *Acts* 4:12.
6 See *Gal.* 1:11 -12.

revelation and His word 'a light unto our path',[1] for it bestows on us the illumination of the Countenance of Christ and so re-fashions our hypostasis.

The struggle of the Christian does not only consist in up-rooting the law of sin from within, but it is intensified for the image of Christ to be engraved in his heart, that image in which he was created in the beginning. Certainly, the image of the Almighty Jesus cannot be imprinted on a heart which is like hard soil trodden down by sins and the passions,[2] neither on a lukewarm heart which does not await a Saviour from Heaven.[3] This is the reason that, within the Church, our struggle is concentrated first on finding and then cultivating the deep heart. In this way, man establishes within his heart a spiritual and divine sensation which renews his life and makes him of great price in the sight of his Creator and Father.[4]

If we are to reach this our desirable aim and know in our heart the Lord Jesus 'risen from the dead',[5] we need to learn from the humble school of the commandments of the Lord. First and foremost, we must embrace the greatest commandment of the Gospel, to consider ourselves as unprofitable servants, even when we have fulfilled all the commandments, since we have done nothing else but 'that which was our duty to do'.[6]

1 See *Ps*. 119:105.
2 See *Luke* 8:5, *Matt* 13:4, *Mark* 4:4.
3 See *Phil*. 3:20.
4 See *1 Pet*. 3:4.
5 *1 Tim*. 2:8.
6 See *Luke* 17:10.

In the Gospel, the Lord set forth love for God unto self-hatred as a condition for man to be His disciple.[1] Just as Christ revealed His love for man through His Passion, Cross and Resurrection, so also man reveals his love for the Lord when he considers himself dust and ashes before God and hates everything in him that is opposed to the mind of Christ. The energy of this hatred uproots the passions from the heart and detaches man from everything created. It replaces the law of sin, which has enslaved the heart, with Christ's law of grace and man thus adopts the 'good and acceptable, and perfect will of God'[2] as the sole law of his being. And, certainly, there is no other will that reigns in Heaven and overshadows the earth except the Divine intent to have all men to be saved[3] and come to know His truth, which will render them genuine and free children of God for all eternity.

Through the act of fulfilling the commandments, man descends to the depth of humility where he meets Christ, crucified out of His love for the world. Having found the Lord as his Fellow-traveller, man then ascends to the height of the vision of the judgments of His spotless love, and this imparts to him a divine state and enlargement to embrace the whole being of mankind from the foundation of the world unto the end of time. Then he brings every creature before God in his prayer of intercession, an act which testifies to his fulfilment as a human hypostasis in the image and likeness of Christ.

1 See *Luke* 14:26.
2 *Rom.* 12:2.
3 See *1 Tim.* 2:4.

Despite the grievous events the Church undergoes throughout history and the tensions among her members, which are all due to the imperfection of human nature, she has nevertheless preserved undiminished her capability of giving birth to images of Christ, that is, to the Saints. She has never ceased to impart inner strength to her members for their regeneration, strength that refashions them into true hypostases which bear divine-human fulness in the likeness of the Hypostasis of the Son and Word of God, in Whom dwells 'all the fulness of the Godhead bodily'.[1]

The Saints intercede for the salvation of the whole world and as perfect imitators of Christ, they reach the last extreme of the commandment of love, which is love for enemies. In this way, they bear witness that the Orthodox Church is the place where the Holy Spirit, the Spirit of Truth, 'bloweth where it listeth',[2] making possible man's spiritual perfection.

On the Sunday of Orthodoxy we celebrate God and the souls that have become His images, gods by the wealth of His grace. The true Church is the one that bears in her bosom these charismatic hypostases with divine-human fulness, with prayer for the whole world and love for all, even for enemies. Such souls are led by the Holy Spirit and bear witness to the world of the true dimensions and perfection of evangelical life which is a foretaste of the eternal Kingdom of the Father and the Son and the Holy Spirit.

1 *Col.* 2:9.
2 *John* 1:3.

Sunday of Saint Gregory Palamas

In the person of Saint Gregory Palamas, the Immaculate Church sets forth the ideal of Hesychasm, in order to intensify the striving of her children, so that they might be graciously adorned for Holy Easter.

Hesychasm is a gift and an ascesis, through which the man of faith stands in the Presence of God with the mind in the heart, calling on the supracosmic Name of the Lord Jesus. In this way, he removes the rust he accumulated in this world which lies in evil, and gathers traces of grace in his heart, healing and uniting all his being.

When these traces of the grace of God reach a certain fulness, the man of faith participates in eternal events, feasting in a godly manner upon the awesome and incomprehensible Passion of the Lord Jesus Risen from the dead, entering into His Living Presence.

The summit of the experience of Hesychasm is the vision of the Light of the Person of Christ, which is the Light of the Resurrection and pledge of the eternal salvation of all those who loved the Name. This vision is the humble Appearing of the Almighty Jesus in our much afflicted world.

Sunday of the Cross

This Sunday celebrates the finding of the Cross by the Empress Helen (c.250 – c.330), so that the holy wood of the Cross might be venerated by the faithful. The Cross of Christ is the commandment that He received from the Father to sacrifice His life for the salvation of the world. Through the fulfilment of this commandment He revealed His love unto the end and reconciled man with the Heavenly Father.

Our Cross, whether small or great, is allowed by the all-wise providence of God in our transitory life. It is precisely the cross that we need, in order to free ourselves from all attachments, which prevent us from following Christ with a free heart wherever He leads us. We become friends of the Cross not only when we believe in and venerate the Cross, but above all when we crucify our mind and heart through faith, in order to fulfil the commandment of Christ in our voluntary journey into the depths of humility. Thus we learn the spirit of Christ's humble love, which becomes within us the power of God and the wisdom of God, an inspiration and consolation in every circumstance of life.The Cross is elevated today in the middle of Lent to strengthen our struggle for spiritual renewal and to lead us into the grace of the Resurrection of the Almighty Jesus.

Sunday of Saint John of the Ladder

Today the Holy Gospel reminds us that without fasting and prayer we are not able to be delivered from the demonic pestilence of sin.

Our immaculate Church also tells us that the fruit of her crucified life are the Saints. A perfect example is Saint John of the Ladder, who teaches us that when we till our heart with the plough of the Cross and guard it with vigilance, we find the Paradise of God within us.

His teaching has a vision which is similar to a submarine, into which not a drop of water can enter. According to this teaching, guarding the mind and the heart from every alien thought or sinful image preserves the benefit of our struggle to attain salvation, which we undertake at all times, but more especially during this period of Holy Lent.

The great Apostle Paul encourages us to not be 'ignorant of the devices of the enemy' (2 Cor. 2:11), but with vigilance to hold our every thought captive 'to the obedience of Christ' (2 Cor. 10:5).

Troparion of the Annunciation

Today is the crown of our salvation

and the manifestation of the mystery

that is from all eternity:

the Son of God becomes Son of the Virgin

and Gabriel announces the good tidings of grace.

Therefore let us also cry aloud with Him

to the Mother of God:

Rejoice thou who art full of grace,

the Lord is with thee.

The Feast of the Annunciation

The feast of the Annunciation is a great consolation which the Church bestows upon her faithful during the time of Great Lent, so that their souls may rejoice in the grace of the words of the Archangel Gabriel to the Holy Virgin: 'Hail, thou that art highly favoured, the Lord is with thee!' (Lk. 1:28).

The Mother of God, of the lineage of David, Prophet and King, had an inner beauty past description, and a rare love for prayer. 'The king's daughter is all glorious within' (Ps. 45:13).

Praying in stillness within the Holy of Holies in the Temple, she gathered the traces of the grace of God in her heart, until she attained to spiritual fulness. Then, by the Providence of God, she read a passage of Isaiah: 'Behold a virgin shall conceive and bear a son and shall call his name, Emmanuel' (Is. 7:14, cf. Mt. 1:23). At these words, divine energy concentrated in her heart, and with all her being she knocked unceasingly at the door of Heaven: 'Lord, make me worthy to be the servant of this woman who will bring into the world the Saviour God, Emmanuel.'

During her fervent prayer, the Archangel Gabriel appeared to her and said: 'Not the servant, but the Mother of Emmanuel herself. Hail, thou that art full of grace, the Lord is with thee. Blessed art thou amongst women.' The Mother of God humbled herself to the state of a servant and God exalted her to divine motherhood:

'For He hath regarded the low estate of His handmaiden [...] He that is Mighty hath done to me great things' (Lk. 1:48-49). For the sake of these great things, according to her prophetic word, she will be called blessed by all generations (cf. Lk. 1:48). We Christians, when we glorify the Virgin now and to the end of the ages, calling her blessed from generation to generation, do nothing other than fulfil this divine prophecy.

Due to the depth of her humility, the Mother of God attracted the charismatic visitation of God and won the highest calling. Pride, full of the evil of self-divinisation, hurled even the angels from heaven to hell. Now, through her humility, the Mother of God empties herself from all creation so as to give space and freedom to God to dwell within her, so that she might rise up to Heaven. If love, the highest of the virtues, 'suffereth long and is kind, ... envieth not, ... vaunteth not itself, ... never faileth' (I Cor. 13:4-8), according to the Apostle Paul, then this is achieved because love is supported and helped by humility. Humility is the way that the Saviour God came down to us, and we are called to become disciples in the school of His humility, so that we may become His own forever.

The Mother of God also had the virtue of being obedient and surrendering to the will of God. In the beginning of creation, God said 'Let there be...' (Gen. 1:3) and all things came into being. Today the Virgin, through her obedience to the word of the Archangel and in spite of all the danger that this entailed as she had not known a man, surrendered to the pre-eternal Counsel of God, saying: 'Be it unto me according to Thy word' (Lk. 1:38). And immediately, the greatest miracle occurred, the Creator Himself descended to earth and renewed all creation.

On the day of the Holy Nativity of the Son of God, the supernatural childbearing of the Virgin made her innocence subject to suspicion and endangered her life. She, however, did not speak to justify herself, but surrendered to God in silence, forcing Heaven to defend and justify her (cf. Mt. 1:20). The Lord brought forth her judgment as the noonday (cf. Ps. 36:6) and glorified her Name.

Today is the beginning of the birth of the Church, because, through the power of the Holy Spirit, the Most High descends to take on flesh from the Holy Virgin, to take on a human Body, which will become the immaculate Church, the Ark of holiness and eternal salvation.

Sunday of Saint Mary of Egypt

As Holy Lent draws towards its close, the Church follows the Lord with wonder and fear on His voluntary path from Galilee of the Gentiles to Judea and onwards to Jerusalem. Her children now intensify their repentance, inspired by the Great Canon of Saint Andrew of Crete and the example of Saint Mary of Egypt.

As a wise Shepherd, Saint Andrew goes through the whole of sacred history in his penitential Canon. The word of Holy Scripture becomes the personal content of man's life and a cry from the abyss of his fall to the abyss of God's mercy. In the person of Saint Mary of Egypt, we discern true repentance which raises the sinner from the depth of corruption to angelic heights. We see in her wondrous life her godly passion of love. We are persuaded by her perfect self-denial that Christ is our ultimate desire and the fulfilment of our every longing.

The love of God is paradoxical, always new and never waning. The humility of the way of the Lord, which extends from the height of Heaven to the earth and even to the nethermost parts of the earth, inspires repentance. This way has the Cross of Christ as its centre. It is referred to in the Gospels as the Cup of Christ.

Christ asks of His disciples the crucial question: 'Are ye able to drink of the cup that I shall drink of, and to be baptized with the baptism that I am baptized with?' (Mt. 20:22). In other words, can they participate in His Cup and His Baptism? The disciples answered: 'We are able' (Mt. 20:22).

In like manner, are we really ready to become partakers of the Cup of Christ's Passion, death and Resurrection? The Cup of Christ contains all the suffering, the frailty, the pain and the tragedy of the world, that is, the death of man, from the creation of Adam until the end of the ages. It is the cup of death which Christ drank in order to heal the wounds of human nature and to ignite the fire of salvation on earth, saving us not through His omnipotence, so as not to frighten us, but through the weakness of His love, which is stronger than the world and death.

Through His Cross and Resurrection, the Lord transformed this Cup of death – preordained for Him by the righteous judgment of the Heavenly Father and held in store for Him by the evil of men – into a Cup of Life and Salvation. Following in our repentance the humble descent of the Lord, we transform the cup of sorrows of this transitory life into a Cup of eternal life from which we drink as his closest friends, becoming drunk with the sober drunkenness of His Divine love. 'I will take the cup of salvation, and call upon the Name of the Lord' (Ps. 116:13).

Lazarus' Resurrection

Troparion

That Thou mightest give before Thy Passion

an earnest of the common resurrection,

Thou hadst raised up Lazarus from the dead,

O Christ our God; and bearing palms

like the children in token of victory,

unto Thee who hadst gotten the victory

over death do we cry:

Hosanna in the Highest,

Blessed is He that cometh

in the Name of the Lord!

LAZARUS COME FORTH

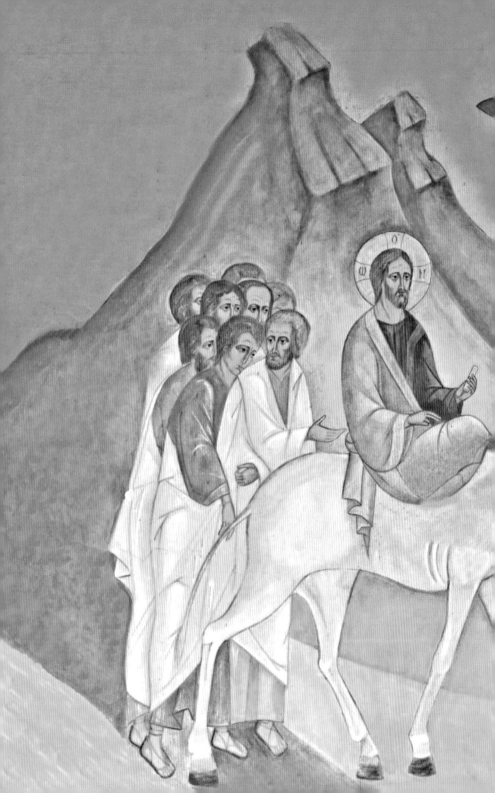

The Entry of our Lord into Jerusalem

This present day is a prophetic event, a glimmer of the glory of Christ which will be revealed in all its fulness at the end of the ages. Today the Lord enters into Jerusalem and the whole city is shaken. On the last day He will come with glory and the entire earth will quake, so that all those things that are shaken may be removed, as things that are made, and only the things which cannot be shaken might remain, marked with the incorruptible grace of the Almighty Jesus.

At His entrance into Jerusalem, the Jews did not apprehend the real identity of the meek and humble Messiah, Who came to them riding on a humble animal, the foal of an ass. We need to learn the meekness and humility of the Saviour God, so that we might know His visitation, and our house may not remain desolate, but through His grace we may stand in His presence and sing, 'Blessed is He that cometh in the Name of the Lord' (Mk. 11:9).

As the children spread their clothing for Christ the Messiah to pass over them and bless them, so we also lay down the impulses of our will and our desires, so that the Lord may rule over our free heart. Then, His grace will overshadow us and we shall become His own forever.

Holy Week:
'It is Time for the Lord to Act'
(Ps. 118:126)

Holy and Great Monday

'Behold the Bridegroom cometh' (Mt. 25:6), and blessed is the servant who will be found worthy to receive His saving visitation and put on an incorruptible crown.

The Church prays in these days that no one remain outside of the Bridal Chamber of Christ, where the awesome union of the heart of man with the Spirit of God takes place.

Saint Paul gives us the key to the Bridal Chamber, saying that the Lord is nigh: we must fill our mind and heart with all those things which are true, honest, just, pure, lovely, of good report, virtue and praise (cf. Phil. 4:8). Such care with regard to the things we allow to exist in our hearts is befitting in view of the One Whom we are encountering there, namely, Him Who for the sake of our salvation went up to Golgotha to undergo suffering unto death.

Only His undying love is able to heal the wretched desolation of our ingratitude. Christ died out of love, yearning to reveal the love of His Father, in the hands of Whom He delivers His Spirit. He dies for man, for whom He shed purging sweat and His life-giving blood. He did not die under an alien law, but under His own.

Holy and Great Tuesday

These holy days we do not just commemorate the Passion of the Lord: through the grace that the Church has bestowed upon us during Great Lent, we become contemporaries of His Passion.

The Lord is the Lamb of God 'slain from the foundation of the world' (Rev. 13:8). He is continually slain for us unto the end of the ages, so that we, His enemies, might enjoy unending delight in the Body and Blood of His covenant.

Today, the Covenant which the Lord concludes with His people is the covenant of His love unto the end. From our side, this covenant demands resistance to sin unto blood. This is the talent with which we trade in a godly manner, so as to acquire the Lord as Saviour and Friend.

Thus we will become His own forever and inherit the boundless freedom of His love, hating only whatsoever opposes it. His love justifies the blameless justice of the Father. His love saves guilty man, so that he is not crushed by His divine and righteous judgement. 'For God so loved the world that He gave His only begotten Son, that whosoever believeth in Him should not perish, but have everlasting life' (Jn 3:16).

Holy and Great Wednesday

The Lord came to send 'fire' upon the earth (cf. Lk. 12:49). As He makes His way towards Golgotha, this fire flares up and transforms whosoever draws near:

Publicans become merciful and give away their possessions; their heart is enlarged fourfold.

Infants are made wise, and perfect a hymn of gratitude to God, Who 'comes meek, humble and having salvation' (Zach. 9:9).

Harlots are made chaste and the madness of their depraved life is turned into insatiable love for God.

The thief is enlightened and becomes an excellent teacher of the justice of the Cross, so that on the very same day Paradise is opened to him.

The mystery of the love of Christ is great and incomprehensible; only a burning heart is able to grasp it even a little. We need a garment of humility in order to come into the quickening presence of the suffering Lord of Glory, and receive the anointing of His saving wisdom.

Holy and Great Thursday

Today is the anniversary of the institution of the Divine Liturgy, which the Lord gave us in a prophetic way before His Passion and sealed with His blood on Golgotha.

The Lord expressed this Covenant through His holy word, saying: 'He that eateth My flesh and drinketh My blood, dwelleth in Me, and I in him. As the living Father hath sent Me, and I live by the Father, so he that eateth Me even he shall live by Me' (Jn. 6:56-57). The terms of this New Covenant of the Lord are the programme of the life of all who have faith and partake of Christ, who will inherit His Unfading Life:

'Ye are they which have continued with Me in My temptations. And I appoint unto you a Kingdom as My Father hath appointed unto Me, that ye may eat and drink at My table in My Kingdom' (Lk. 22:28-30). Let us ask the Lord to take us with Him to His Passion, to teach us the humble ethos and silence of the Lamb of God which put Pilate to shame. Let us implore Him to give us perfect surrendering to His holy will, that He may lift us onto His Cross and take us down to the tomb within His heart, so that we may become the content of His heart, rise with Him, and belong to Him for ever.

Holy and Great Friday

The Lord cries out on the Cross for our sake, 'My God, my God, why hast Thou forsaken Me?' (Mt. 27:46), so as to heal our apostasy from His grace. Each of us, full of awe before the utter humility of the Lord, cries with gratitude: My God, my God, why have I forsaken Thee, unjustly and senselessly? Thou O Lord, though it would be just, do not abandon me, ungrateful as I am.

'Greater love hath no man than this, that a man lay down his life for his friends' (Jn. 15:13). Christ kept silent on the Cross for a little while, so that by His silence He might speak more clearly to the sons of men about the mystery of the ways of His salvation.

By the Cross of the Lord we mean the affliction, deprivation, illness, humiliation, suffering and agonising death that is allowed by the judgement of God. We do not choose our cross, but as the Lord Himself accepted the Cup of the Wisdom and of the judgements of the Father, so we also surrender ourselves to His holy Providence. In order to enter into life, we have to pass through death following the Lord.

Lament me not, O Mother

Lament me not, O Mother,

when thou beholdest

in the sepulchre thy son,

whom without seed

thou conceivedst in thy womb,

for I shall rise again

and shall be glorified;

and forasmuch as I am God

I shall exalt in glory everlastingly

those who in faith

and love magnify thee.

Holy Saturday Matins, 9th Ode

Today, Christ descends into the tomb
clothed with the robe of the curse of sin,
and having as the content of His heart
His love to the end for the salvation of the world.

Tomorrow, He shall rise from the tomb,
leaving behind that shroud which the wickedness of men
imposed on Him and which the righteous judgment of God
allowed, granting redemption and eternal salvation to all
sinners, which He loved to the end.

Holy and Great Saturday

When Christ enters the universe He bears within Him the pre-eternal will of the Triune God: to save all the world from the condemnation of death. He makes known to everyone the word of His Father without Beginning. He prays in Gethsemane with sweat like drops of blood for all Adam. He suffers His awesome Passion bearing in His heart the desire for the salvation of all. He ascends on the Cross and descends into the grave with the same intention and yearning.

He descends to the nethermost parts of the earth, so as to sanctify all the created world and to give us the power to meet Him in whatever situation we find ourselves, whether in joy or pain, hope or despair.

And all that, due to His undying love: because God so loved the world that He gave His only-begotten Son, that no one should perish who believes in Him (cf. Jn. 3:16).

The fire of His perfect love dissolved the seal which was put upon His grave and His holy Tomb opened, in order that the righteous Son of God should not see corruption.

Christ does not save us by the almighty power of His Divinity, but through the weakness of His Holy Flesh with which He drew nigh to man so as to impart to him all the wealth of His gifts. His ascent and His glory were natural attributes of the Son and Word of God. His descent to hell, however, is an even greater miracle, because through it He hides His glory in order to manifest His perfect love, which saves man from whatever hell he has been cast into by sin. Through our love and gratitude for His goodness, we become heirs of His undying Life. God's love is ineffable, unspeakable. Even the Word of God Himself, in order to express it perfectly, fell silent on the Cross: 'Father, forgive them. They know not what they do.' Heavenly love is concealed within earthly enmity, so that it vanquishes it through death and ensures life within love, dissolving all darkness and the shadow of death.

'For God so loved the world that He gave His only begotten Son, that whosoever believeth in Him should not perish, but have everlasting life.' It is as if the angels engraved on the tomb an epitaph, unfitting for any mortal until then, but which, from then on, became common for all mortals who believe in Christ: 'O death where is thy sting? O hell, where is thy victory?' (1 Cor. 15:55).

'A little leaven leaveneth the whole lump' (Gal. 5:9). And the newness of life, that is grace upon grace, which springs up from the grave, transforms the entire nature of man, so as to make him fit for the blessed Kingdom of God, where, as an Angel, he will live eternally with his Saviour God.

Holy Pascha: The Resurrection of our Lord and God and Saviour Jesus Christ

'Fear not; I am the First and the Last, I am He that liveth, and was dead; and, behold, I am alive for evermore' (Rev. 1:17-18). These are the words of the Risen Christ to His beloved disciple, John the Theologian. These words describe the path of the Lord, but also of man, which goes through death and leads to eternal life.

The Lord loved mankind with a perfect love. He died for all who were condemned to death because of the ancestral sin. The unjust death of the Lord became a condemnation of the just death of all men, bestowing upon them eternal salvation. 'Christ is risen from the dead, and there is none left dead in the tomb' (Sermon attributed to Saint John Chrysostom, *Paschal Midnight Service*). The more righteous and in accordance with Christ's commandments, the more perfect will be the condemnation of death in his person, that deadening which man bears within him, and the more certain his entrance into the Living Presence of the Risen Lord.

This is what the Lord desired to convey with His evangelical word: 'Only when the grain of wheat falls onto the ground and dies, will it sprout and bring forth much fruit' (Jn. 12:24).

The sufferings of this life, when they are endured without sin, with faith, and even with gratitude, condemn the death we have inherited through the sin which preceded.

For this reason precisely, the Apostle suggests as a program of life: 'Remember Jesus Christ raised from the dead' (2 Tim. 2:8). That is, we need to remember that for us to become partakers of the victory of Christ over death, we have to follow also the example of His path, constantly tasting death in order to keep alive the sensation of His Presence within us. Thus we will put to death any sinful malice which would hinder His Spirit from dwelling within us. This paradoxical in-dwelling is the earnest or pledge of the better resurrection which we await.

Every movement through which we draw nigh to the place of the Living Presence of Christ is for us the eternal Easter.

Our entire life becomes a journey: from despondency to godly desire, from darkness of ignorance to the light of the knowledge of God, from the narrowness of self-love to the enlargement of Divine Love, from the slavery of sin to the freedom of the children of God, from temporal death to imperishable, never-ending life, from earth to heaven, from man to God.

Christ, as Righteous and Sinless,

Is Risen from the dead,

By death, voluntary and without cause,

He hath overcome death - the wages of sin
(cf. Rom. 6:23)

And to them in the grave

Hath He given everlasting Life,

As a pure gift of His Love.

The angel cried

The angel cried
unto Her who is full of grace
O pure Virgin rejoice!
And again I say rejoice,
thy son is risen
the third day from the tomb
and hath raised up the dead,
be glad O ye people!

Shine, shine O New Jerusalem
for the glory of the Lord
is risen upon thee!
Rejoice now and be glad O Zion
and do thou rejoice,
O pure Mother of God,
for the fruit of thy womb
is risen again!

Easter Matins, 9th Ode

Pentecostarion:
Waiting for the Promise of the Father
(cf. Acts 1:4)

'That your joy might be full' (Jn. 15:11)

During the period of the Triodion, we prepared for the great event of the Resurrection of the Lord Jesus, so as to receive the first grace, the first portion of the Holy Spirit, as the Apostles did, when the Risen Lord appeared to them and breathed upon their faces saying 'receive ye the holy ghost' (Jn. 20:22). The time of Triodion is like a path for us to approach the Lord leaving behind the vanity of the world. The end of this path, the meeting with the Lord, is for us the eternal Easter, the Kingdom of all ages of which the King is Christ Himself.

The joy of the Resurrection strengthens us to continue with the struggle of salvation, which is rather the struggle of co-operation with the Lord for a sublime creation: the creation of small gods from the great God, Who is risen from the dead. Our battle is not yet finished, we have seen the truth of Easter and the joy we felt was real but not yet permanent or final. 'I will see you again,' says the Lord, 'and your heart shall rejoice, and your joy no man taketh from you' (Jn. 16:22). It is not yet final, because in this life everything is unstable and can be shaken. The joy which we feel on Easter night is like an explosion, but we still await 'the great and terrible day of the Lord' (Joel 2:31), when He will come to give permanence to all the promises that He has made to us. In the same way that Christ strengthened His disciples 'giving in their hearts the earnest of the Spirit' (2 Cor. 1:22), Easter imparts the grace to strengthen us within the Church, as we live in expectation of an even greater fulness of our communion with God.

The day of Easter, as we see in the Acts, marks the beginning of a new era in the history of the salvation of man. Eternity overshadows time and the Kingdom of God breaks through into the life of the faithful within the Church. The Lord commanded His disciples 'that they should not depart from Jerusalem, but wait for the promise of the Father' (Acts 1:4). According to Christ's prophecy, that the Shepherd would be smitten and the sheep scattered (cf. Mk. 14:27), the disciples had previously dispersed. But quickly, coming to themselves, they ebbed back and, regaining their strength they united together again. Deprived of the Teacher, they transformed their grief into fiery prayer. This was the beginning of this intense period of the expectation of the promise of the Father, the gift of the Holy Spirit.

The disciples were gathered together with one accord in prayer and supplication (cf. Acts 1:14), as if they had one soul. As they awaited the Lord, the Mother of the Lord strengthened them by her presence (cf. Acts 1:14) in a dignified and quiet way. What word could she say? She lent her flesh to God and gave us the greatest Word, Her son, the hypostatic Word of the Father. All of the disciples, and the Mother of God, had the same longing, the same prayer, the same intense expectation, believing in the promise of Christ, that the heavenly Father will send another Comforter, the Holy Spirit to guide them 'into all truth' (Jn. 16:13). The nature of the disciples was to be strengthened and sanctified with the descent of the Holy Spirit, so as to bear all the fulness of grace, all the fulness of the holy love of God.

When the Comforter comes, He does not speak of Himself. He is a hidden visitor, a mystical friend, Who announces all that Christ has spoken, bringing it to remembrance. The Holy Spirit comes to communicate to us the gift, the charisma of Pentecost, which unites us with Christ eternally. No one can be a member of the Church of Christ, unless they have a spiritual gift.

The fire of the gift that we received in Holy Baptism, and of the chrism of the Holy Spirit sealed on all the members of our body, is reignited at Pentecost. In Baptism we put on Christ, in whom dwells 'all the fulness of the Godhead bodily' (Col. 2:9), and we accept Him in our heart. However, Baptism on its own is not enough, if we leave it in the past and do not act upon it in our present lives. Moreover, we must continuously nourish and increase the Lord within us through the Mystery of Holy Communion and through tears wrought by the spirit of repentance and gratitude, so that this 'investment' of grace will remain alive and be preserved active and saving until the end

Our Holy Church trains and guides us spiritually through the themes which it expounds every Sunday during the period between Easter and Pentecost. In the period of the Triodion, we are given a 'constant' every week, a principle which like the laws of physics will be proved true with perfect precision, so as to help us to establish within us the law of God, and enable us to find the deep heart and receive the grace of the Risen Lord. Similarly, in the period of the Pentecostarion, through the Gospel and Epistle readings, the hymns and troparia, we are gradually initiated into the mystery of the gift of Pentecost, the mystery of life-bestowing unity with the head of the body of the Church, who is Christ. The content which we are taught has as its purpose to create a firm base on which we can step safely in order to make the great leap of faith and receive the gift of the Holy Spirit which will lead us into His Kingdom.

The period of the Pentecostarion prepares us to have living contact with the Lord, in order to receive in our heart the fiery flame, the gift of the Holy Spirit. This tongue of light, like the hot iron which engraves letters on wood, will carve on our heart the image of the Lord Jesus Christ. This furthermore is the prayer of the Church, that Christ be formed in our hearts (cf. Gal. 4:19), that His icon may be painted in an invisible, immaterial way, so that we may know that we are not alone, but united with Him in Whom we believe and to Whom we belong. Then we become 'taught of God' (Jn. 6:45), according to the Evangelist John. We see our heart and that is enough to bring us into contrition and humility, to bring us gratitude and to constantly renew our inspiration for prayer and our longing for greater and deeper union with the Author of our salvation, the Almighty Jesus.

The constants which we are given each Sunday of the Pentecostarion will build up a longing, expectation and faith in us which will not be shaken even before death. Through these constants, and with all these ideas, we will draw nigh to the feast of Pentecost and the Lord will find us fit and ready for the grace of the Comforter, the Holy Spirit, the Spirit of truth, which will create in us apostolic hearts, full of a fervour of love towards Christ, full of the light of the knowledge of God; hearts which bear within them every man from the beginning until the ends of the ages, making intercession for them all. This is the enlargement of the heart, the gift of Pentecost.

Thomas Sunday

The first Sunday after Easter is called the Sunday of Antipascha or Thomas Sunday. The Gospel reading describes the appearance of the Lord to His disciples, eight days after the Resurrection. Thomas, who was absent when the Lord appeared to them for the first time, doubted their witness. He wanted to see and touch in order to believe. When the Lord said to Thomas: 'reach hither thy finger, and behold my hands; and reach hither thy hand, and thrust it into my side' (Jn. 20:27), even before Thomas touched Him, as the Fathers say in their commentaries, he entered into the presence of the Risen Christ, crying out 'My Lord and my God!' (Jn. 20:28). We could almost say that Thomas was the first person who received the gift of speaking in tongues: when the power of salvation, the power of the Risen Lord entered his heart, he offered up this sound, 'My Lord and my God!' (Jn. 20:28).

The gift of speaking in tongues was a unique gift which God gave in the beginning of the life of the Church with the coming of the Comforter. When people felt the entry of the Spirit of God in their heart, they made wordless utterances of joy, thanksgiving and glorification. They knew only that their God had enveloped them in His Spirit. In the beginning, speaking in tongues was thought of as a great gift because everyone was strengthened in faith. Later, however, the Apostle Paul demoted it to the bottom of the list of the gifts of the Holy Spirit. Moreover, he deterred them from exercising this gift when they were together (cf. 1 Cor. 14:27-28).

Consequently, the gift of speaking in tongues was superseded by noetic prayer, the unceasing invocation of the Name of Christ. In other words, the faithful found another means to cultivate their heart, and keep the living feeling of Christ in their midst, so that they no longer needed the gift of speaking in tongues. The spirit of gratitude is so strong that the man who surrenders himself to it becomes delirious and makes wordless sounds which he cannot express before others, because that would usurp their space. However, when we are in our chamber (cf. Mt. 6:6) we offer to the Lord hymns and entreaties with 'groanings which cannot be uttered' (Rom. 8:26).

We see that God permits Thomas to waver, so as to teach us the mysteries of His Kingdom. Through his providential and blessed doubt he makes known to us the true law of faith (cf. Rom. 3:27): 'Blessed are those who have not seen and yet have believed' (Jn. 20:29). We are always blessed when we base everything on the promise of God. Whether we see Him within us, or we do not see Him, our trust remains undiminished and we cleave to His commandments and to His Spirit without suffering change. This is the law which the Church gives on Thomas Sunday, rekindling the words of the Lord.

In everyday life, 'Blessed are those who have not seen and yet have believed' (Jn. 20:29) applies to all of us. We are those who have seen the grace of the Resurrection as the troparion says, but we are also those who must be tried in order that our true heart be revealed. Each of us is one who has seen and believed, and one who has *not* seen and yet believes. All of us who have come to the Church have been given in the beginning a great grace to unite with Him. It was as if we saw Him wholly alive in our heart, so following Him was effortless. We were even able to accept insults from others without reacting, without putting them in their places, without demonstrating our intelligence and superiority. When the Lord was present in our heart we were ready to humble ourselves, eager to pray, and the memory of God could not leave us, either while sleeping or waking. His words were so sweet in our heart and on our lips, that we wanted to continuously study the Scriptures.

And so, the ascents which the Lord puts in our hearts in this period have no end. Afterwards, however, God permits us to be tried and withdraws this palpable grace. As grace diminishes, often it ebbs away so far that we feel complete dryness. Then, however, our true heart and our true intention will be revealed.

For as Gregory Palamas says, 'Dishonour has tried the heart.'[1] Dishonour, provocation which we receive from someone, the dryness we feel when grace is removed from us, or the pain

1 Saint Gregory Palamas, *The Homilies*, edited and translated from the Original Greek with an Introduction and Notes by Christopher Veniamin, Mount Thabor Publishing, 2014, p. 12.

that we suffer when we are tried in this life, will reveal our true heart. We are blessed if we hold on to the lesson the Lord gave us through the experience of His Resurrection.

If in this period of desolation and dryness, we refer the same prayers to God and remain standing with the same faith before Him giving Him glory, honour and righteousness, taking upon us the shame and offence, then we are blessed because we are 'as seeing Him who is invisible' (Heb. 11:27). We offer to God what we used to offer to Him when we saw Him wholly alive in our heart. We have a need, all of us, to hold onto this principle because nothing in our life is permanent. Many times we descend deep into the netherworlds. A few times, God will again raise us up high through His comfort and the power of His grace. But we must steadfastly keep the lesson that has been given us by this grace.

In this way we learn to employ every art and detect every humble thought which will bring us closer to Christ, so that this second period of the spiritual life becomes creative. Independently of whether we feel the presence of God in our lives or not, we maintain the firm faith that the Lord is true, and has shown forth His truth through His life and death. It ceases to have meaning for us whether we see Him and He regenerates us with His presence, or whether He withdraws and we feel death approaching us through the deprivation of His countenance.

What is the really important thing? It is not whether we suffer, whether our desires are fulfilled, whether we live, whether we die (cf. Rom. 14:8). The only thing that is important is that we know that He is risen from the dead, that we find contact with Him and are well-pleasing to Him, following His commandments. For us He remains God, blessed and good unto all ages, and we are His servants forever. Such faith overcomes the world and shares in the victory of the Risen Christ (cf. 1 Jn. 5:4).

Sunday of the Myrrhbearers

The Myrrhbearers, that is, Mary the Mother of Jesus, Mary Magdalene, Joanna, Salome, Mary the wife of Cleopas, Susanna, Mary and Martha of Bethany, were women dedicated to Christ, who because of their great love for the Lord, stood before the empty tomb and felt the presence of Him Who was risen. The empty tomb was enough to speak in their heart so they might believe in the Resurrection of their Beloved Teacher.

This day has a beautiful lesson for us. We read in the Gospel that at the terrible hour when the Lord gave up His last breath hung upon the Cross and all was overshadowed by the threat of death – the Apostles being affrighted and scattered because of the terrible events which had taken place – Joseph of Arimathea, ignoring any threat, found the courage and boldness to present himself to Pilate and ask for the body of the Lord Jesus. The Gospel gives us in a few words a characterisation of Joseph which has great significance. He was someone who 'waited for the Kingdom of God' (Lk. 23:51), he believed in the God of Israel, who came and will come again and he expected His Kingdom. This faith and anticipation of the Kingdom gave him the courage to present himself before

Pilate, endangering his life. When the Lord said that the Kingdom of God is within man, He meant to speak of Himself, coming to dwell in the hearts of all those who love Him.

In the case of Nicodemus also we witness a wondrous change. In the beginning, 'he came to Him by night' (Jn. 3:2) with fear and shame to confess Him publically. Now, regenerated from his conversation with the Lord and by the spirit of His living presence, he becomes like a lion and boldly comes with Joseph to bury the dead body of Jesus. Likewise, also our own heart must burn with the expectation of the coming of the Lord, Who came, Who dwells with us until the end of the ages, and Who is coming again to judge the living and the dead. If we have this expectancy of the coming of the Lord Jesus, we will be, even us, strong and courageous to take on every work of devotion so as to be well-pleasing to God.

Man needs the faith of the heart that 'worketh by love' (Gal. 5:6), which we have been taught about on the Sunday of Thomas, and the expectation of the Kingdom of God, so that he keeps his inspiration. In other words, in order that his inspiration remains constant and increasing, he must have always before his eyes the coming of the Lord and await Him in suspense. The first Christians had great inspiration because they awaited the appearance of the Lord. His coming was for them impending at any moment. For this they prayed saying, that the grace should come and the world pass away. They knew that the grace of Christ is the Kingdom of God and they had such a longing for this coming, that they finished their prayers saying, in the Aramaic language, *Maranatha*, that is, *Come, Lord* (cf. 1 Cor. 16:22). They did not await His coming passively, with inertia, but they called Him to hasten. Not only did they call Him to come quickly but as the Apostle Peter writes in his Epistle, they hastened unto the coming day of the Lord (cf. 2 Pt. 3:12), running towards this appearance of God, so that His presence comes unto them sooner. The expectation which they had of the Kingdom of God, which they understood as the presence of the risen Christ, was so powerful, that it overshadowed everything and gave them the courage to be led even to martyrdom. Faith was made firm on earth through the blood of the martyrs, and by their prayers and intercessions. This faith of the martyrs has reached all the way to us, in spite of the fact that we are in a poor state, lacking their intensive expectation for the Kingdom of God and simply abiding in the Church in peace.

Through the Sunday of the Myrrhbearers we are taught that if we have ardent desire for the Kingdom of God and expect the imminent judgement of the Lord, then we will never become despondent, but we will always renew our inspiration. Our yearning and expectation to unite with the Author of our salvation, Christ, means everything to us.

Every time the sublimity of Christian life which He brought to the earth is set out in the Holy Scriptures and in all the three great Apostles, Paul, John and Peter, it is immediately related to His Second Coming, as a means for the inspiration and power which is needed to acquire this perfection. The boldness which is given by the expectation of the Promise of God, strengthens man to have perfect self-denial and confidence in the gift of God, in order to be led into all truth (cf. Jn. 16:13) – into all the fulness of the love of Christ (cf. Eph. 3:19), Who is the true Paradise and fulfilment of the life of all reasonable creatures.

As Christians, we approach the great and final feast of Pentecost with expectation and rekindled longing for the gift of the Holy Spirit, the fiery flame of the Comforter, which the Lord gave on this day. Through this gift we will escape the corrupting vanity of the world, the suffocating deception of its values, and the ensnaring delusion that the illusory loves of this world are compatible with the spotless love of God. Through this gift, the Holy Spirit will remind us of the quickening words of the Almighty Jesus (cf. Jn. 14:26) and will keep us united with all the Saints, who yearned for the appearing of the One Who has come and will come again (cf. Heb. 10:37). For they endured with pain and struggle, so that they might be crowned and come into the supernatural and wondrous feast of Heaven, into the Light of the Presence of the Father and of the Son and of the Holy Spirit.

Sunday of the Paralytic

On the Sunday of the Paralytic, we hear the Lord ask the paralysed man who has been infirm for thirty eight years, a paradoxical question: 'Wilt thou be made whole?' (Jn. 5:6). Many times the Lord conversed with man so as to provoke faith in His word, and then to perform the miracle of His goodness. The Lord certainly knew that the paralysed man had remained close to the pool of the Sheep-gate awaiting a miracle and cure. However, out of respect for our freedom, He never does anything without our consent and collaboration. Everything is accomplished through the collaboration of two factors, the divine, which is infinitely great and the human which is infinitely small, but absolutely necessary. His will, which is that 'all may be saved' (1 Tim. 2:4), is given. Subsequently, everything depends on how our will responds. Nothing is passive, nothing happens by the will of God alone, although also nothing can happen only by the will of man, because without Him we can do nothing (cf. Jn. 15:5). He is overcome by the desire to hunt our heart, but this depends on us, on whether we open its door.

When Christ asks this question, 'Wilt thou be made whole?' (Jn. 5:6), He wants to stir up desire and a strong intention in the paralytic for the restoration of his health. The Lord endeavoured to stir up in him the desire for healing and, furthermore, encouraged him to express his desire to be made whole. In the same way, the Church 'at sundry times and in divers manners' (Heb. 1:1) stirs up in the faithful the desire for the gift of Pentecost, in order that they may unite with the glorified Body of Christ, with 'all the saints' (Eph. 1:15) in heaven and His elect on earth. The Church impels the faithful to express this desire through prayer.

Healing follows on from acquiescence to the Comforter, as we see when the paralytic offers himself to be healed. However, later on when the Lord meets him in the temple, He says to him, 'Behold, thou art made whole: sin no more, lest a worse thing come unto thee' (Jn. 5:14). A great problem arises at this point: how can we keep the grace which we have freely received from God Who is good? It is as if He says to the former paralytic, 'You have received the grace of healing which you sought. If you want to preserve it within you, from now on try to surrender yourself to the will of God, and live a crucified life on the earth, dead to the passions of the world and to sin.'

Every day, with a deep sense of our uselessness, we seek healing from the paralysis of the passions and despondency, for His grace is the only power which is able to bridge the 'great chasm' (Lk. 16:26) between our world and the much longed for Kingdom of God. The Lord who is most-merciful and ready to reconcile, answers to our plea and gives us His grace, but in order to preserve it we must cease from sin and live in submission to His holy will. When we taste of a small death, through the fulfilment of His commandments, we enter into His life-giving presence. Remembering Jesus Christ risen from the dead (cf. 2 Tim. 2:8), we can also say, 'I was dead and behold I am alive for evermore' (Rev. 1:18). In this way, the life of the man of faith is well-pleasing to God who constantly enriches it. Man who was the laughing stock of the demons, becomes eternal delight for Him who redeemed him with His precious Blood, the Lord Jesus Christ.

This miracle revealed the messianic and divine identity of the Lord Jesus. All miracles have as their source and cause the greater miracle, which is faith, when it is accompanied with the conforming of our small and feeble will with the great and perfect will of God. In this period, the immaculate Church strives to rekindle our longing and expectation for the gift of Pentecost. Today's Gospel reading brings into relief a spiritual law, exemplified in the patience and faith of the Paralytic: 'God's gifts are given *without fail* to each of us (cf. Mt. 7:7-11) but according to the measure of our thirst and faithfulness to the Bestower: to some more, to others less abundantly.'[1]

---

1 *We Shall See Him as He Is*, p.180.

Mid-Pentecost

In between these Sundays we celebrate Mid-Pentecost, when the Church speaks to God through the troparion of the feast, with an upsurging cry:

'In the midst of the feast give my thirsty soul to drink of the waters of godliness, for Thou didst cry unto all O Saviour, if any man thirst let him come unto Me and drink, O Christ our God, wellspring of Life, glory be to Thee.'

Here the Holy Church exhorts her children to continue in the expectation of the promise of the Father which the Lord gave us, and intensifies their thirst for the gift of the Holy Spirit which is to come on the day of Pentecost. In essence, this thirst is no more than a little echo of the anguish caused in us by the 'fire' (Lk. 12:49) which the Lord came to spread over the earth. It is our response to Jesus' great zeal for our salvation, which did finally eat Him up, when He cried out in the middle of the Feast:

'If any man thirst, let him come unto me, and drink. He that believeth on me, as the scripture hath said, out of his belly shall flow rivers of living water' (Jn. 7:37-38).

'As the scripture hath said' means the true faith 'which was once delivered unto the saints' (Jud. 1:3) on the day of Pentecost. In reality, 'as the scripture hath said' refers to whatsoever the Lord Jesus said about Himself, as the true Messiah and Saviour of the world, the Son of God.

In the second chapter of the Gospel of Saint John, Christ says about Himself that He is the true temple of God not made by hands (cf. Jn. 2: 19-21), in which His human nature was united indissolubly and without confusion with His Divine Nature. In the third chapter, He says that He is the true fiery serpent (cf. Jn. 3: 14-15), whose sight saves from the poison and spiritual death of sin. In the sixth chapter, He describes Himself as the true manna, the bread of life (cf. Jn. 6:58), which comes down from Heaven giving life and fulness to the hearts of men. In the seventh chapter, Christ refers to Himself as the true rock out of which comes living water (cf. Jn. 7:37-38). In the eighth chapter of the same Gospel He certifies that He is *He that is*, the Lord – 'I AM THAT I AM' (Ex. 3:14) – Who revealed Himself unto Moses and Who was before Abraham (cf. Jn. 8:58): the One 'which is, and which was, and which is to come, the Almighty' (Rev. 1:8). We find manifold such descriptions of the Lord in His Gospel.

This is the true faith which will beget the insatiable longing for the gift of Pentecost and will make known the Divine origin of the Lord Jesus. This longing is the measure and the true worth of each man in the sight of God and in the expectation of His salvation. It is with such longing and with such thirst that man approaches the Mystery of Holy Pentecost. The ascension of man's longing meets the condescension of God's mercy, so that the greatest miracle in the life of the world may come to pass: the union of the heart of man with the Spirit of the now known and beloved God. The thirst for the promise of the Father inspires one to ascend the ladder of Christ's Beatitudes unto the last step of spiritual perfection and of the rich entrance into the Kingdom of the Father, and of the Son, and of the Holy Spirit, of the great and true God of love.

'Fill my soul with the living water of godliness, which is the Holy Spirit', the Church cries with an apocalyptic voice, and asks God to quench her thirst by the gift of the Holy Spirit.

Sunday of the Samaritan Woman

The Sunday of the Samaritan Woman expresses this thirst for 'the well of water springing up into everlasting life' (Jn. 4:14), the grace of the Holy Spirit which renewed her life, transformed her impropriety, and made her an Apostle of the Lord with 'rivers of living water' (Jn. 7:38) flowing from her heart. We learn that thirst for God and for His gifts is of the highest importance, so that we may be found worthy of life-giving communion with Christ, Who is for us the true entry into His Church, that awesome place where His spirit reigns. The Church is indeed an awesome place, because it is not simply what we see: it is a mystical communion with the Risen Lord, the head of the body, through the Holy Spirit.

The Gospel reading about the Samaritan woman reveals the way of Christ Who, as He said, did not come to be served, to dominate, to rule, but to serve and give His life 'as a ransom for many' (Mt. 20:28). The maker of heaven and earth meets the Samaritan woman, who was a sinner and an enemy of Israel, and puts Himself below her, seeking help from her, as if He had need of her, so that she might feel honoured. It was not accustomed for a Rabbi to speak to a woman and the disciples show surprise when they find Him talking to her.

This shows even more Christ's humility. His presence is life-giving, His word is revelatory and His humility, patience and kindness transform her heart. The Samaritan woman feels honoured, acquires the beauty of dignity, and opens her heart to the life-giving words of the Lord which transform her life. She humbles herself so she can receive the prophetic rebuke of the Lord, and, soon after, one of the highest teachings of the Gospel: 'Woman, [...] the hour cometh, and now is, when the true worshippers shall worship the Father in spirit and in truth [...]. God is a Spirit: and they that worship him must worship him in spirit and in truth' (Jn. 4:21-24).

The sacred lesson which the Lord teaches the Samaritan woman with great meekness remains for all eternity: 'God is a Spirit and they that worship him must worship him in spirit and in truth' (Jn. 4:24). God is worshiped only through the Holy Spirit. No one can even pronounce the Name of the Lord Jesus without the Holy Spirit, as the Apostle Paul states (cf. 1 Cor. 12:3). Christ is the truth, as He Himself said 'I am the way, the truth and the life' (Jn. 14:6). His truth is made known in His humble way, as He revealed it to us. Thus all who want to truly venerate the Father without beginning, must follow Christ's way of descent, the way of humility and love, which is engraved in the commandments which He left us. Worship that is worthy of God must be offered to God 'in spirit and truth' (Jn. 4:24). From the side of God, this is realised through the Spirit of Truth, Who proceeds from the Father without beginning and dwells in the deep heart of man. From the side of man, this is realised through the spirit of truth, which characterises him as a man of faith, when he repents with prophetic self-knowledge and humility, seeing himself as God sees him, and continuously learning what he lacks. He thirsts and yearns for God with all his being.

Christ emptied Himself and descended into the netherworlds of the earth, filling the depth of the abyss with His grace. The heavenly Father however, raised Him up and gave Him the Name before which 'every knee should bow' (Phil. 2:10) and all creation worships. He accepts whomsoever follows His way as the inheritor of His life. In order to be well-pleasing to God and have a sanctified and life-giving relationship with Him, let us follow His example, giving our fellow the first place and putting ourselves below every creature, as our Holy Fathers have taught us. Then our heart will slowly be enlarged, our fellows will be informed by grace, and God will be glorified by the life and the presence of the Spirit which ever increases amongst His own. Man becomes true and attracts the Spirit of Truth, the Holy Spirit, through the spirit of contrition and humility. Imitating the Lord, he puts himself below others and makes all those who come in contact with him share in his gift. Christians who have this attitude in worship proceed with steadfast gait towards the last and great feast of Pentecost, awaiting with strong expectation its gift, the promise of the Father.

Sunday of the Blind Man

In the Gospel of the blind man, as also in that of the Samaritan woman, we see the importance of true knowledge of God and right dogma for the transformation and enlargement of the heart. We urgently need to acknowledge our poverty and blindness, our ignorance of the mystery of our beloved God, in order to not fall into delusion and to keep our inspiration alive.

As Christ Himself said, the purpose of this healing was to manifest His glory and to transmit to men true knowledge of Him. The negative reaction of the Pharisees to His creative work and their refusal to receive Him as the 'great light' (Mt. 4:16) from above, provoked the Lord to pronounce 'For judgment I am come into this world, that they which see not might see; and that they which see might be made blind' (Jn. 9:39).

God created man with a specific purpose: to become a partaker of His glory (cf. 2 Pt. 1:4), to reflect it in all creation and to return it back to Him, its source. As the Apostle Peter says, 'ye should shew forth the praises of Him who hath called you out of darkness into His marvellous light' (1 Pt. 2:9). God is the great light and man is His reflection. When the Lord came in the flesh, he did not want to accomplish anything of Himself (cf. Jn. 8:28), but only the work which the Father commanded. He did not seek His own glory, but the glory of Him who sent Him (cf. Jn. 8:50). Thus also man, as the mirror of the glory of God, should not reflect anything of himself, but only that which has been given to him from above, neither should he try to hold onto anything for himself, but return everything to God with thanksgiving.

The Pharisees based their confidence in their knowledge of the law and their virtues. For this reason, they failed to discern the heavenly light which illumines and enlarges the heart of all men. The man who was born blind, by contrast, showed forth his simplicity and sincerity. Thus he was deemed worthy not just of bodily vision, of which he had been deprived until then, but moreover of spiritual vision, confessing Christ as the Lord of all.

Faith in Christ and the confession of our sinfulness, which is the only real darkness, cleanses the mirror of our soul so that we can reflect the Light of Life, the Lord. If we put our faith in any kind of physical gift, it dulls the surface of the mirror and can no longer reflect the light. The soul should not take as its light something from itself, that is, something created, but rather should reflect the Light of God, which is uncreated. Only then does man truly follow Christ and gain the light of life.

From the moment when the Son of God came into the world, He became a point of reference for all mankind. He is a sign of God for all generations, 'which shall be spoken against' (Lk. 2:34). Eternal salvation, or eternal redemption, depends on how man defines himself before Him. Infidelity leads to the darkness of death, but faith in Him has eternal life as its inheritance.

Many people approached the Lord during the days of His life on earth. The multitude thronged Him, but only a few found life-giving contact with Him, like Joseph of Arimathea, Nicodemus, the Samaritan woman and the blind man. Others saw, heard, left, and still they remained the coarse crowd which one day cried 'Hosanna to the Son of David [...] Hosanna in the highest' (Mt. 21:9) and the next, 'Crucify him' (Mt. 27:22,23). If we do not come close to the Lord with faith, devotion, fear and humility, then we can not unite with His spirit.

We draw nigh to the temple of the Lord, which is full of His glory and grace, but how many of us find that contact which leaves us regenerated, renewed, like the Jews drunk from consolation, singing 'we were like them that dream' (Ps. 126:1)? How many of us will leave as if drunk from the comfort which we find when we become one with the living hope of our salvation, Christ?

The healing of the man which was blind from his birth reminds us in many ways of God's creation of the universe from nothing. Through this healing, the physical health of the blind man was restored. However, when he later recognised the Lord as his Benefactor, he was also healed spiritually, for he received the supernatural gift of faith and inherited the life of heaven.

If we thank God continually from our heart for the life which He has given us and for all His benefits towards us, we will then justify His gift and graciously provoke His goodness to also bestow upon us His supernatural gifts, through which we may be well-pleasing unto Him and fulfil our pre-eternal purpose.

God always grants His supernatural gifts in proportion to the gratitude and thanksgiving with which we receive them. Whatsoever we present to God as coming from Him, becomes truly our own. As we are enriched by God through ceaseless thanksgiving, we also become partakers of the gifts of the Saints and our elect brethren in Christ, when we offer up thanksgiving to God for the gifts with which He has endowed them. When we become 'thankful' (Col. 3:15), which means people of thanksgiving, as we have described above, then we are guided from the darkness of ignorance into the light of all the truth of God (cf. Jn. 16:13) and, in a way that is befitting, we glorify Christ, Who has become for us the source of every good thing.

Ascension Troparion

Thou art ascended in glory

O Christ our God,

gladdening Thy disciples

by the promise of the Holy Spirit;

for they were assured

through Thy blessing

that Thou art the Son of God,

the Redeemer of the world.

The Wondrous Ascension of Our Lord, Prophetical Event of His Glorious Second Coming

This same Jesus, which is taken up from you into heaven, shall so come in like manner as ye have seen him go into heaven (Acts 1:11).

For forty days the Lord 'showed himself alive' (Acts 1:3) unto His disciples. He was instructing them through His Presence, but He was at the same time training them through His absence, increasing their thirst for a more perfect union with Him, for a union in the Holy Spirit. Although before they had known Him according to the flesh, from now on they were going to know Him in the Spirit. 'It is the Spirit that quickeneth,' and now 'the flesh profiteth nothing' (Jn. 6:63).

The disciples had known Christ Incarnate and lived with Him so closely, that He had told them: 'Henceforth I call you not servants... but I have called you friends' (Jn. 15:15). Now, however, the disciples, having come to believe in Christ's Resurrection, needed to know that Jesus is the Lord of Sabaoth and that their love and relationship with Him had to be in the Spirit. This is the reason why the risen Lord said to Mary

Magdalene: 'Touch me not' (Jn. 20:17). She also had to move beyond her joyous experience of seeing Christ's risen body in order to begin to relate to Him through the Holy Spirit.

Ascension is an especially prophetical event. In His last conversation with the Apostles, the Lord referred to the end of the ages, when His Kingdom would be restored in glory. The Apostles could not yet perceive the magnitude of this restoration, limiting it only to the people of Israel. It is on the day of Pentecost, when the Holy Spirit descended on them, that their hearts were perfectly enlarged to embrace the universal salvation of Christ.

The Lord ascended as He was blessing the Apostles. 'While he blessed them, he was parted from them' (Lk. 24:51). In the Book of Acts it says that He departed from His disciples in the same way in which He will appear on the day of His Second Coming (cf. Acts 1:11). As the Lord says in His Gospel (cf. Mt. 25:31-32), when He comes He will gather His own from all the ends of the earth, so as to receive them into His Kingdom. And what will the voice of His goodness say unto His elect in that dreadful hour? 'Come, ye blessed of my Father, inherit the kingdom prepared for you from the foundation of the world' (Mt. 25:34). We see that the Lord ascends into Heaven while blessing, and He will bless even more apparently and more richly His elect on the last day of His Second Coming.

A cloud received him out of their sight' (Acts 1:9). The Lord ascends to the heavens in glory. In the Old Testament, the cloud of light – the glory of God – was continually accompanying His Presence. In the days of His life on earth, however, He concealed His glory so as to be able to draw nigh to us and prepare us, that His own glory may also become our inalienable inheritance. When the Lord was taken up into heaven, the angels explained to the disciples the significance of the event, bearing witness that He will come again with the same glory on the last day (cf. Acts 1:11). Angels now rejoice in the ascent of the Saviour into Heaven and armies of angels will also minister with power and triumph the great event of His Second Coming.

The event of the Ascension of the Lord occurred in a sudden unexpected manner, while He was speaking to His disciples. The Almighty Jesus, Who has in His power the times and the seasons, warned us that He would come again at the end of the ages, suddenly and unexpectedly, 'as a thief in the night' (1 Thess. 5:2). The day of the Lord must be unexpected, because in this way it will clearly reveal those who have true love for Him Who has come, that is, those whose heart is awake even as they sleep, longing for the beloved Bridegroom of the Church and their God, those who have enough oil of grace in their vessels to keep their lamps alight, as we are taught in the Parable of the Ten Virgins (cf. Mt. 25:1-13) and in the lives of all the Saints.

Sunday of the Fathers of the First Ecumenical Council

Today we celebrate the Holy Fathers of the first Ecumenical Council convened in the city of Nicaea in AD 325, who established in a dogma that the Lord Jesus Christ is true God, the Son of God by nature, and not a created being as was argued by the Arians.

After all the previous weeks, the Church warns us on this day that without faith in the Lord Jesus Christ as true God and Saviour of the world, we cannot become partakers of the gift of the Holy Spirit. The close disciples of the Lord - Peter, James and John - first confessed by the mouth of Peter the Divinity of Christ (Mt. 16:16), that He is the Son of the Living God, the true Messiah, and only after were they able to see His glory on Mount Tabor. It is the same with us: without the right faith in Christ we are unable to receive the gift of the Holy Spirit. Without the right faith, the salvation and knowledge of God are impossible.

The Gospel reading for this Sunday (Jn. 17:1-13) includes part of the High Priestly Prayer which Christ offered to the heavenly Father just before His Passion. When the Lord had accomplished His work of salvation, He sealed it with this prayer, asking the Father that He also seal it with His divine glory for the salvation of the whole world. It provokes awe to hear Him make intercession, not just for His disciples, but for all who would accept His teaching and follow Him to the ends of the ages. In His words we feel the zeal which ate Him up for our sake and we see His exceeding sorrow unto death (cf. Mk. 14:34) for the salvation of the world. 'O Righteous Father, the world hath not known Thee: but I have known Thee' (Jn. 17:25). The Church thus reminds us that the gift of Pentecost is the fruit of the prayer of the Lord Jesus 'with strong crying and tears' (Heb. 5:7) and certainly also of His unfathomable sacrifice. Our desire and thirst for the Holy Spirit can never be enough, therefore we need to put all our trust and hope in the life-giving Lord.

After the Ascension of Christ, the Holy Apostles were living in great tension, continuing with one accord in prayer and in breaking of bread (cf. Acts 1:14; 2:46), because the Lord had promised them that He would send 'another Comforter' (Jn. 14:16) – the promise of the Father, the Holy Spirit – Who would guide them 'into all truth' (Jn. 16:13), into all the fulness of the love of Christ (cf. Eph. 3:19). The Lord had promised His disciples that He would not leave them orphans (cf. Jn. 14:18). Nevertheless, He was taken up into glory and for a short period of ten days the Apostles did, in a way, remain orphans. This happened in order to increase the intensity of their expectation and prayer, that they might become even more receptive to the gift of the Holy Spirit and that when the day of Pentecost would be fully come (cf. Acts 2:1) they might experience the great earthquake of the true knowledge of God.

At Pentecost the tongues of fire call all men to unity and thus fulfil the entreaty that Christ had presented to God the Father in His high priestly prayer: 'Holy Father, keep through thine own name those whom thou hast given me, that they may be one, as we are' (Jn. 17:11).

With the coming of the Comforter another wondrous word of the Lord is fulfilled: namely, the exhortation He addressed to Nicodemus: 'Ye must be born again' (Jn. 3:7). The gift of Pentecost illumines man with the light of Christ and, while he still lives on earth, he tastes 'the powers of the world to come' (Heb. 6:5). Though he is still clothed with flesh, he already breathes the air of the Heavenly Kingdom. His transitory life is overshadowed by eternity and then he indeed knows the true God and worships Him 'in Spirit and in truth' (Jn. 4:24).

The purpose of this Sunday is to instil in us the same tension which the Apostles had, and to stir up our thirst and expectation for the gift of the Holy Spirit, so that we also may receive the fiery flame of the Comforter on that great day of the Feast. That when we shall hear the words 'the day of Pentecost was fully come' (Acts 2:1), the Church may become heaven and we – citizens of Paradise, members of the glorified Body of the Lord Jesus Christ.

Pentecost Troparion

Blessed art Thou

O Christ our God,

Who didst endue

the fishers with wisdom,

sending upon them the Holy Spirit,

and through them

didst draw the world into Thy net.

Glory be unto Thee,

O Lover of mankind.

The Feast of Pentecost

T he great Mystery of Pentecost is foreshadowed in the life of the Prophet Elijah. He sought the Face of the Almighty Lord with great zeal on Mount Horeb, where wondrous and awesome events took place. First, a strong wind rent the mountains, breaking the rocks in pieces. Then came a strong earthquake followed by fire, but the Lord was not in them. Finally, there came a 'still small voice' and therein was God (1 Kgs. 19:11-12).

Pentecost fulfils the prophecy of Joel, wherein God promises to pour out His Spirit upon all men: 'I will pour out my Spirit upon all flesh; and your sons and your daughters shall prophesy' (Joel 2:28). On this day, while the Apostles prayed, 'there came a sound from heaven as of a rushing mighty wind', then 'cloven tongues like as of fire' descended and sat upon each of the disciples of Christ, filling them with the Holy Ghost, so that they spoke in other tongues of the 'wonderful works of God' (Acts 2:2-4,11).

The fiery tongues illumined the minds of the Apostles with the light of the knowledge of God and warmed their hearts with the power of the love of Christ so that they might stand in His Living Presence.

We see, then, from the feast of Pentecost and its foreshadowing in the life of the Prophet Elijah, that the Spirit of the Presence of the Lord comes after a 'rushing mighty wind' and a prophetic earthquake. In the same way, the Holy Spirit breaks through in the life of the faithful so as to regenerate them, causing an earthquake and stirring up a mighty wind in their conscience, which helps them realise the vanity of all the things of this world, and the death of sin that separates them from the Living God of love.

True faith does not bring despair, but entreats with the language of the prayers of Pentecost: 'Ere we return to the earth, vouchsafe that we may return unto Thee; and do Thou receive us in Thy favour and grace [...]. Set over against the multitude of our transgressions, Thy boundless compassion' (*The Great Vespers of Pentecost, Kneeling Prayers*).

True faith has its confidence in the gift of God and is inspired by the humble ethos and spirit expressed in these prayers: 'Against Thee only have we sinned, but Thee alone do we worship. We know not to bow down before strange gods, neither have we stretched out our hands, O Lord, to any other god.'

When the Spirit comes, He will witness to the Divinity of Christ and will give man godly power for the saving invocation of His Name: 'And it shall come to pass, that whosoever shall call on the name of the Lord shall be delivered' (Joel 2:32).

The first gift which the Holy Spirit gives to the regenerated soul is prayer of the heart:

> Lord, according to the years wherein
> the pestilence of sin has wasted us,
> the vanity of the world has withered us
> and the mist of our treachery has deluded us,
> come and freely fill our hearts
> with the incorruptible consolation of Thy Spirit,
> so that we, as of old Thine apostles,
> may know the awesome resounding
> of Thy Divine Love,
> and discern of which spirit we are,
> receiving the seal of Thine inheritance,
> our great God and Saviour,
> with all the Saints who have loved Thine Appearing.
> Amen.

Monday of the Holy Spirit

'If I go not away, the Comforter will not come unto you; but if I depart, I will send him unto you. And when he is come, he will reprove the world of sin, and of righteousness, and of judgment: of sin, because they believe not on me; of righteousness, because I go to my Father, and ye see me no more; of judgment, because the prince of this world is judged' (Jn. 16:7-11).

When the Holy Spirit comes, He will enlighten man to know that everything which happens without reference to Christ God and without faith in Him is sin. 'For whatsoever is not of faith is sin' (Rom. 14:23). Only the Holy Spirit reveals sin and only He can abolish it.

The Holy Spirit also reveals the true righteousness and justice of God, as Christ expressed it on the Cross: 'Father, forgive them; for they know not what they do' (Lk. 23:34). True justice means to endure suffering for the sake of the commandments of God, while being innocent. As Christ was sinless, His suffering was unjust and it thus became a condemnation of death which was just in our case, because of the sin which preceded. Likewise, every pain and hardship which we undergo in order to be reconciled with God condemns sin and eradicates death in our flesh. Thus, it is through the Cross that joy and salvation came into the world.

True judgment occurred through the self-emptying and utter humility of Christ (cf. Phil. 2:7), by which the prince of this world was overcome (cf. Jn. 16:11). When the man of faith takes upon himself the blame for his injustice and ingratitude, he anticipates the final judgment, receiving remission of sins and grace from the Holy Spirit. For this reason, those who are led by the Holy Spirit never cease to blame themselves before God and to humbly prefer the will of the other.

When all the hard sayings of the Gospel are accepted with faith, they crush the arrogance of man, so that through the paradoxical power of contrition and tears he might come to know the incorruptible consolation of the Holy Spirit which follows the earthquake of repentance: 'Blessed are they that mourn for they shall be comforted' (Mt. 5:4).

The Name of Christ, the words of the Holy Scriptures and the Mystery of the Divine Eucharist all become one life, through the grace of the Holy Spirit, in the heart of the regenerated man. The power of this life ceaselessly transfigures and renews him so he may fulfil the 'good, and acceptable, and perfect, will of God' (Rom. 12:2). The great mystery of Pentecost is at work in every Liturgy. We offer bread and wine, gifts in which we have invested all our life; and we request and entreat the Heavenly Father to send the Holy Spirit and transform them into the Body and Blood of Christ, filling them with

His Life which is without beginning. We continue, more and more intensely, to pray that our participation in the Holy Gifts will be 'unto the communion of the Holy Spirit' (*The Divine Liturgy*). When we are vouchsafed to hear the heavenly voice saying: 'The holy things unto the holy', and to partake of them, then we will be blessed to exchange our small and corruptible life with infinite and divine Life. This is the reason that in the end of the Liturgy we chant a song of victory: 'We have seen the true Light, we have received the heavenly Spirit, we have found the true faith, we worship the undivided Trinity: for the same hath saved us.'

When the Holy Spirit enters the heart as a rushing mighty wind, crushing its hardness, there, in the deep heart, He depicts the image of the Lord Jesus Christ. He will transform and purify our heart, so that we can invoke the Name of the Lord from the depths.

The purpose of our life is the acquisition of the Holy Spirit and in this the Lord encourages us through His divine words: 'If ye then, being evil, know how to give good gifts unto your children: how much more shall your heavenly Father give the Holy Spirit to them that ask him?' (Luke 11:13).

My Lord Jesus Christ,

Thou art a good Comforter

and Thou dost bring consolation unto life.

Do not leave me desolate and dead,

deplorable and sinful as I am.

As in the beginning, O Creator,

Thou gavest living breath to clay,

likewise now by the grace of Thy Spirit,

revive my life paralysed by despondency.

Bring, O Lord, the good breath of Thy Spirit,

upon our dry and cold bones

that we may live and know that Thou art Lord

and God and Saviour of our souls.

Three Gifts of the Holy Spirit

The readings from the Old Testament during the Vespers of this feast speak prophetically about three gifts of the Holy Spirit.

The first is the gift of prophecy. When the Holy Spirit comes, men shall prophesy. This means that they will be able to receive and pronounce words of eternal truth.

The second gift is the grace given to man by the Holy Spirit to invoke in a godly manner the Name of the Lord and thus to be saved. We know from the Apostle Paul that 'no man can say that Jesus is the Lord except by the Holy Ghost' (1 Cor. 12:3), and from the Apostle Peter that, 'there is none other name under heaven given among men, whereby we must be saved' (Acts 4:12).

The third gift is that God will give man a heart of flesh on which the law can be engraved with the spirit of the commandments of the Gospel. This spirit was expected to come into the world in the last days, when Christ would appear on earth.

When the Holy Spirit descended on the Day of Pentecost, these three promises were fulfilled.

Firstly, the disciples prophesied with a lofty spirit. Secondly, they spoke in strange tongues, which was later succeeded by the gift of noetic prayer of the heart. Thirdly, through this gift, they were able to cultivate the inner man, embracing the word of God as their own nature.

The Apostle Paul writes that 'every man has his proper gift' (1 Cor. 7:7), which is requisite for him to be incorporated into the Body of Christ, the Church.

Repentance is the first among the fundamental gifts in the life of the Church, as it is both introductory and inclusive of all the other gifts. Through repentance, man is reconciled with God and preserved from sin.

The second gift is humility, which is absolutely necessary for man to be initiated into the Mystery of Christ, as the Lord says: 'Learn of me; for I am meek and lowly in heart' (Mt. 11:29).

However, the gift which ascertains the authenticity of all the other gifts and intensifies zeal for 'the increase of God' (Col. 2:19) is continual thanksgiving from the heart. According to the measure of this gratitude, the Lord Christ renders His gifts to His faithful servants. Everything for which we continually give thanks to God ultimately becomes our own. When we thank God for His suffering and His sacrifice, salvation is made ours. Then God Himself becomes our inheritance.

The purpose of our life is to acquire a small flame. This flame is a spiritual pain in the depth of our soul that reminds us continually of 'Christ and Him crucified'.[1] Then all our thought and concern is how to be pleasing to the Lord, Who lived, died and rose again for our sake. For us, He descended and ascended, and He gave us as an inheritance the gifts of the Holy Spirit. Let us ask the Lord to give us 'a small flame of the Comforter, cool and refreshing', which will engrave in our heart the image of Christ and will guide us into all the truth of His Love.

1 *Cor.* 2:2.

Sunday of All Saints

All the Saints are the fruit of Holy Pentecost. As the Holy Spirit descended to earth to witness to the Divinity of Christ and to reveal His image, so all the Saints witness in the Church to the Divinity of the Holy Spirit and manifest His image.

After the ascent of the Lord above the Heavens, the Heavenly Father was well-pleased with the work of His Son, and the gifts of the Holy Spirit rained upon the earth. Wherever they found good soil, they brought forth fruit of holy life. All the members of the Body of Christ, who are united with the Head and with each other, bear gifts of grace.

God foresaw that no one on earth, however holy, would be able to bear all the wealth of His gifts. Thus He perfected a Body in history, to which He imparted all His gifts. Every member is joined to the Body through their 'proper gift' and enriched by partaking of the gifts of all the other members, of all the Saints. All the members of the Body of Christ, who are united with the Head and with each other, bear gifts of grace. The salvation of Christ is full and wondrous in this communion of grace within His Body. No one can conceive of the height and depth, the

breadth and length of the ineffable love of Christ (cf. Eph. 3:18), unless they are in communion with all the Saints.

It is dangerous to reject even one Saint, for then the whole choir of the Saints will reject us also. On the contrary, there is great wisdom and understanding in acquiring friends from the citizens of the Heavenly Zion, that they might receive us on that great and holy day of our departure from this life to the God of our Fathers.

The Eternal 'Today' of the Church

Every liturgical act is an initiation into the mystery of time. In Divine Worship we become contemporaries of eternal events. At every feast we hear the word 'Today': 'Today is the crown of our salvation', 'Today the Virgin gives birth to Him Who is above all being', 'Today hell groaning cries out', 'Today He Who hung the earth upon the waters is hung upon the Cross'. Though these events do not recur in time, we experience them through the grace of the Holy Spirit as present and contemporary.

All the events of the divine Economy, as for example the Nativity, the Crucifixion, the Resurrection and the Second Coming, are recapitulated in the Person of Christ. Partaking of divine grace we are united with Christ and become contemporaries of these historic events. Through His grace we come into contact with eternity. Living with expectation and longing for the feasts of the year, the time of our life is transformed into a continual feast, into a time of rejoicing and succour. The 'today' of the feasts and each 'today' of our transient life becomes to us the earnest of the goodness of God which is given to us so that we can co-work with Him and build up our eternal being, 'redeeming the time'.[1]

1 *Eph.* 5:6.

This is the purpose of the Church: to meet the eternal God within finite time. Every time that we gather in the Name of the Lord in order to delight in His quickening word and celebrate the memorial of His saving Passion, according to His indisputable promise the Lord is Present, bestowing upon us His eternal grace. Thus, through the Holy Mysteries, through the feasts and through prayer, the imperishable energy of God overshadows the time of our life and marks it, sealing it with eternity. Finally, time itself will come to an end, because it will be swallowed up by eternity.

Elder Sophrony spoke about the 'abundance of life' granted us in Christ relating the journey of our spirit to the Banquet of Divine love. He writes 'When Christ's great love touches our heart and mind, then our spirit in the flame of this holy love will embrace all creation in compassionate love, and the feeling of transition into divine eternity acquires invincible strength.'[1]

Since Christ is the fulness of time and recapitulates all things in His Person, when we unite with Him and find contact with His saving energy, the ends of the world come upon us, according to the Apostle Paul (cf. 1 Cor. 10:11). This 'end' will come, of course, at the Second Coming of the Lord, but we see that in the saints it is already at work from this life. The term 'eschatology' is often interpreted as referring exclusively to the Second Coming of the Lord and to the life to come. However, eschatology, as understood and experienced in the Ortho-

---

1 *On Prayer*, p. 103.

dox Tradition, also refers to all the salutary and eternal events of Christ's life on earth, which were accomplished once and for all in the power of the eternal Spirit.[1] By means of the worship and Sacraments of the Church, man becomes a participant in these events already from this life and receives a foretaste of eternity within finite time, even the event of His great and glorious Second Coming, which by its nature pertains to meta-history or more precisely, the supra-historic.

Christ revealed to us the perfect image of the Triune God.[2] In every contact with Him, in every Sacrament of the Church, we are given this fulness of grace, but we are often unable to preserve it. We need time to prepare our vessel to assimilate it. Saint Paul speaks of 'the increase of God' (Col. 2:19), 'till we all come ... unto the measure of the stature of the fulness of Christ' (Eph. 4:13), to which we attain when we 'perfect holiness in the fear of God' (2 Cor. 7:1). Only thus can we be clothed with Christ, with the luminous garment of His glory.

According to the word of the Apostle Paul: 'As many of you as have been baptized into Christ have put on Christ' (Gal. 3:27). Only in this way can a new, charismatic life begin in us which follows the current of His holy will. The grace of God is not a static reality, but a dynamic one, and for this reason we need to preserve it within us by keeping His commandments and partaking of the Mysteries of the Church, which unite us with Him and with one another in the most palpable way.

1 *Heb.* 1:3.
2 See *John* 1:16.

Thus the time of this transitory life is nothing other than the continuation of the goodness of the Lord for us, the gift of His grace so that we may co-work with Him. It is a time of initiation into God's eternity, which is given to us so as to prepare for our Great Meeting with our Lord and Saviour Jesus Christ. Therefore, our life on earth is a time of collaboration between the will of God and the will of man, between Giver and receiver, and this collaboration aims at fulfilling the pre-eternal purpose of the Creator, which is the deification of His reasonable creature.

Above all, time is a mystery which contains the goodness of the Lord, the lovingkindness of our Maker and Deliverer. It is given to us so that, through ascetic effort, we may discover its content and fulness, which is the grace of eternal salvation. The mystery of time is granted to us by the goodness of our Lord, Who is pleased to come and meet us every time we seek His Face. And when we do achieve this blessed meeting, then, according to the Apostle Paul, upon us the ends of the world are come (cf. 1 Cor. 10:11).

Let us, therefore, redeem the brief span of time with which God has entrusted us, raising our eyes to Him at every moment of our life, invoking His Name. Then each 'today' brings us into contact with eternity and opens before us new horizons, revealing the true meaning of time. Thus, every day becomes an opportunity for us to make a new beginning in our struggle, to perfect holiness and to accumulate grace, so that all the time of our life be crowned with the crown of glory and eternal salvation. Our purpose is to bridge the abyss between the image of God in which we were created and the likeness unto Him for which we were destined. This is, in fact, the only perspective able to bring salvation. If we look at our life through this prism, it becomes most precious because it has been redeemed by the unblemished, spotless and life-giving love of Christ, which is the end of the law (cf. Rom. 10:4).

If we exploit the time of the goodness of God, each day will be overshadowed by His wondrous energy and the fleeting time of our life will be transformed into eternal life. The desire and prayer of the Church is that the image of Christ may be formed in the hearts of all men and to reveal the true meaning of time. Then, having delighted in the great mercy and the saving grace of our Lord, they will all render Him the due thanksgiving unto the ends of the ages.

Index of Illustrations

Front cover: *Christ Seated upon a Rainbow*, detail of *The Last Judgement*, fresco on lime plaster, W: 82cm, H: 82cm. Mural, 1998-1999. Chapel of All Saints, Stavropegic Monastery of St. John the Baptist, Essex, UK.

p. 7: *Prophet Elijah Praying in the Cave*, ink and pastel on paper, W: 14cm, H: 16cm. Private collection.

pp. 18-9: *The Nativity,* oil paint on gypsum plaster, W: 2.95m, H: 2.95m. Mural, 1980-1990. Refectory.

pp. 36-7: *The Theophany*, oil paint on gypsum plaster, W: 2.92m, H: 2.87m. Mural, 1980-1990. Refectory.

p. 48: *The Presentation of our Lord in the Temple,* egg tempera on gesso, W: 55cm, H: 43cm.

pp. 58-9: Prayer in Gethsemane, egg tempera on gypsum plaster, W: 2.49m, H: 1.89m. Mural, 1997-1998. Hylands Refectory.

p. 117: *The Annunciation*, egg tempera on gesso, W: 85cm, H: 1.15m. Royal Doors, 1998-1999. Chapel of All Saints.

pp. 126-7: *The Resurrection of Lazarus*, fresco on lime plaster, W: 1.10m, H: 1.28m. Mural, 1998-1999. Chapel of All Saints.

pp. 128-9: *The Entry into Jerusalem*, oil paint on gypsum plaster, W: 1.98m, H: 1.78m. Mural, 1980-1990. Refectory, Stavropegic Monastery of St. John the Baptist.

pp. 144-5: The *Apostles Heavy with Sleep*, detail of *The Prayer in Gethsemane*, egg tempera on gypsum plaster, W: 2.49m, H: 1.89m. Mural, 1997-1998. Hylands Refectory.

pp. 148-9: *The Crucifixion*, egg tempera on gypsum plaster, W: 1.76m, H: 1.69m. Mural, 1997-1998. Hylands Refectory.

pp. 150-1: *Taking Down from the Cross*, fresco on lime plaster, W: 1.46m, H: 1.79m. Mural, 1998-1999. Chapel of All Saints.

pp. 152-3: *Angels Carrying the Body of Jesus*, ink, watercolour and pastel on paper, W: 51cm, H: 11.5cm. Private collection.

pp. 158-9: *Angel Engraving an Epitaph*, ink and pastel on paper, W: 21cm, H: 29.7cm. Private collection.

pp. 160-1: *The Resurrection*, fresco on lime plaster, W: 1.89m, H: 2.88m. Mural, 1998-1999. Chapel of All Saints.

pp. 168-9: *The Virgin Flanked by Angels,* fresco on lime plaster, W: 2.55m, H: 2.30m. Mural, 2003. Hylands Guest House, Stavropegic Monastery of St. John the Baptist.

pp. 206-7: *The Ascension*, oil paint on gypsum plaster, W: 2.95m, H: 2.95m. Mural, 1980-1990. Refectory.

pp. 216-7: *Pentecost*, oil paint on gypsum plaster,

W: 2.95m, H: 2.95m. Mural, 1980-1990. Refectory.

pp. 222-3: *The Holy Trinity*, oil paint on gypsum plaster, W: 3.60m, H: 2.95m. Mural, 1980-1990. Refectory.

pp. 236-7: *All Saints*, egg tempera on gypsum plaster, W: 6.71m, H: 2.83m. Mural, 1997-1998. Hylands Refectory.

pp. 248-9: *Angel Rolling up the Heavens*, ink and pastel on paper, W: 21.0cm, H: 29.7cm. Private collection.

All line drawings: ink and pencil on paper. Private collection.